Legal Essays

LUC JORGART

Copyright © 2024 Luc Jorgart

All rights reserved.

ISBN: 9798320090917

CONTENTS

1. Cyber Hate Crime in the UK from a Legal and Criminology Perspective - A Discussion of Regulations, Suggestions and the Impact of the COVID-19 Pandemic. (English Criminal Law) — Pg1

2. The Liberian Civil Wars: Was There a Breach of International Human Rights Standard in Relation to the Rights of Children and Ethnic Genocide? (International Human Rights Law) — Pg16

3. The Second Amendment, A Polarized Opinion. (American Law) — Pg29

4. Law and Development in the Korean Peninsula: Can the North and South Reach Legal Compromises? (International Law) — Pg37

5. A Comparison of Internet Service Provider Obligations for National Security Reasons - China and England. (Comparative Law) — Pg50

6. A Comparison of Japan and The United Kingdom - What Allows for a Valid Termination of Employment? (Comparative Law) — Pg56

7. The Legal History of Burakumin Discrimination in Japan. (Japanese Law) — Pg65

8. The Okinawan Right to Self-Determination – Problems Presented by the United States Military Presence and a Flurry of American Human Rights Abuses. (International Human Rights Law) — Pg77

9. Comparing Legal Inheritance Principles in Japan and England: Priority Laws, Property with No Valid Inheritor and the Instance of an Inheritors Death. (Comparative Law) — Pg94

1 CYBER HATE CRIME IN THE UK FROM A LEGAL AND CRIMINOLOGY PERSPECTIVE - A DISCUSSION OF REGULATIONS, SUGGESTIONS AND THE IMPACT OF THE COVID-19 PANDEMIC

Introduction

In this paper, I'll be discussing cyber hate crime from legislative and law enforcement perspectives. Cybercrime has been divided into two categories known as cyber-enabled and cyber-dependant crimes. It must first be established whether hate crimes taking place in the cyberspace are cyber-enabled or cyber-dependant crimes.

Cyber-dependant crimes are defined by the Crown Prosecution Service as crimes that can only be committed only through the use of Information and Communications Technology devices. In these cases, the devices must be both the tool of the crime and the target of the crime[1]. Whereas the Crown Prosecution Service defines cyber-enabled crimes as traditional crimes which may be increased either in reach or scale by the use of Information and Communications Technology devices[2].

One academic debated that cybercrimes are new wine with

---

[1] The Crown Prosecution Service, 'Cybercrime - prosecution guidance.' <https://www.cps.gov.uk/legal-guidance/cybercrime-prosecution-guidance>

[2] The Crown Prosecution Service, 'Cybercrime - prosecution guidance.' <https://www.cps.gov.uk/legal-guidance/cybercrime-prosecution-guidance>

no bottle[3] meaning that cybercrimes are a brand-new category of crimes, whilst some may debate this to be true, it is widely accepted that it is only true for crimes that could be classified as cyber-dependant. Another academic describes cybercrimes as "old wine in a new bottle"[4] and this is accepted to be an accurate description for cyber-enabled crimes. Because hate crime offences have existed long before the age of computers, it is safe to say that cyber hate crime offences classify as cyber-enabled offences and not cyber-dependant offences.

An Overview of Cyber Crime Offences

There are many different types of cybercrime offences. One such cyber-dependant offence is unethical hacking. This is where someone gains unauthorised access to a website or database with the intent to either damage, steal virtual property or leave evidence of a virtual break in. This offence is a problem because it can cause the leaking of many people's personal data as well as financial damage to both companies and people. In fact, in June 2021, the GCHQ cybersecurity boss stated that extortion by hackers is the biggest online threat to people inside of the UK[5].

Most types of Cybercrimes are vastly different. One such type of cyber-enabled cybercrime offence is cyber harassment. This is where cyber criminals use the internet or other ICT devices to bully on messaging services, threaten people and post threatening videos. This offence also poses a problem because they can cause people to fear

---

[3] Wall D. (1999) 'Cybercrimes: New Wine, No Bottles?'

[4] Grabosky P. (2001) 'Virtual Criminality: Old Wine in New Bottles?'

[5] (Dan Sabbagh, 2021) 'Ransomware is biggest online threat to people in UK, spy agency chief to warn' - The Guardian 14 June 2021

attack in their daily lives, worry about their safety and can cause mental health problems for the victims. In fact, in February 2020, an MP was subjected to constant malicious messages which she says caused a serious impact on her wellbeing and made her feel like she was being constantly watched[6].

The Prevalence of Cyber Hate Crime

In the year ending March 2020, there were a recorded 105,090 hate crimes in England and Wales (excluding Greater Manchester)[7]. This is a recorded 8% increase from year ending March 2019.

A 2019 study has shown that 30-40% of people in the UK have witnessed some form of online hate speech or abuse and that between 10-20% of the UK population have been personally targeted by online hate speech or abuse[8]. This was reinforced by a recent poll conducted by the British Future think tank in which they found that 13% of White people say that they have been subjected to racist insults on social media, the figure rises to 19% for people from the Pakistani ethnic group and 22% for Black people[9].

In order to combat the prevalence of online hate speech, the Crown Prosecution Service and the courts have begun

[6](Adam Everett, 2020) 'Councillor sentenced for harassment of MP Helen Jones' - The Warrington Guardian 17 February 2020

[7]Home Office, 'Hate Crime, England and Wales', 2019-2020 <https://www.gov.uk/government/statistics/hate-crime-england-and-wales-2019-to-2020/hate-crime-england-and-wales-2019-to-2020>

[8]How much online abuse is there? A systematic review of evidence for the UK. <https://www.turing.ac.uk/sites/default/files/2019-11/online_abuse_prevalence_full_24.11.2019_-_formatted_0.pdf>

[9]Katwala,S , (2021), 'Race and Opportunity in Britain: How can we Find Common Ground?', British Future, UK

to impose harsher sentences on those who commit online hate crimes. In 2019 when the Crown Prosecution Service applied for sentence increases to take into account the aspect of hate within the crime, the requests were granted 77.5% of the time. This is a great leap in comparison to the mere 2.3% that was granted in 2007/2008[10].

An Overview of Criminological Theories

One criminological theory which could relate to cyber hate crime is the 'broken windows' theory. This theory introduces the idea that if people are introduced to an environment where everyone else litters, breaks windows and takes no care of the neighbourhood, they will likely soon behave in this way also because it is what is socially accepted[11]. The same could potentially be applied to the cyber space, if one finds themselves surrounded by nothing but twitter users harassing a celebrity, they may come to accept it as the normal behaviour for the platform and may even join in.

Another criminological theory which could possibly apply to cyber hate crime is the routine activity theory. This theory states that crime is likely to occur when three elements are present: a motivated offender, a suitable target and an absence of a capable legal guardian[12].

---

[10]The Crown Prosecution Service, 'Proportion of hate crime cases getting increased sentences at all time high.'
<https://www.cps.gov.uk/cps/news/proportion-hate-crime-cases-getting-increased-sentences-all-time-high>

[11]Wilson, J. and Kelling, G., (1982) Broken Windows. The Atlantic.
<https://www.theatlantic.com/magazine/archive/1982/03/broken-windows/304465/>

[12]Cohen, Lawrence E.; Felson, Marcus (1979). "Social Change and Crime Rate Trends: A Routine Activity Approach". American

However, this theory traditionally applies to crimes that take place in the physical world and not within the cyberspace. Because of this, there are many questions such as whether or not the routine activity theory can be applied because there is a divergence in space and time between the victim and the offender. The Cyber Lifestyle Routine Activity Theory has been put forward as a solution to these questions and argues that the meeting in space and time of the offender and victim is not the only the only opportunity for potential victimisation within the cyberspace[13].

Another criminological theory that could be applied to cyber hate crime is Jack McDevitt and Jack Levin's 2002 study in which they categorised hate crime motives into four distinct categories. These categories are: 'thrill-seeking' in which the offender engages in hate crimes purely for excitement and drama, 'defensive' in which the offender engages in hate crimes out of the belief they are protecting their communities, 'retaliatory' in which the offender engages in hate crimes out of a desire for revenge and 'mission offenders' in which the offender engages in hate crimes out of ideological reasons. During their study, they found that 'thrill-seeking' accounted for 66% of all hate crimes in the United States[14]. This is particularly worrying as the anonymity of the cyber-space could allow for thrill-seeking offenders to commit crimes constantly and potentially without being caught.

Sociological Review.

[13]Bradford Reyns, Billy Henson and Bonnie Fisher, (2011) 'Applying the Cyberlifestyle Routines Activity Theory to cyberstalking victimization'

[14]Levin, J. and McDevitt, J., (2008) Hate Crimes.
<https://jacklevinonviolence.com/articles/HateCrimesencyc92206FINAL.pdf>

Legal Essays

A Discussion of Cyber Hate Crime Offences

In 2007, a definition for hate crime was agreed upon by the Prison Service, the police and the Crown Prosecution Service. It was defined as a criminal offence which is perceived by the victim or another person as motivated based on a certain characteristic of the victim such as race or disability[15].

The Home Affairs Select Committee has previously stated that ethnic minority female MPs are particularly vulnerable to online harassment and bullying[16]. There are also countless incidents of both footballers and celebrities speaking out about being abused for no reason other than their race, religion or status. One example of this is that in March 2021, the footballer Theirry Henry stated that he would quit using social media until tech companies do more to remove both racism and bullying. He stated that "the sheer volume of racism is too toxic to ignore"[17]. Furthermore, research has shown that ethnic minorities are disproportionately affected by online trolling as well as cyberbullying[18].

---

[15]Hate Crime, England and Wales, 2019-2020
<https://www.gov.uk/government/statistics/hate-crime-england-and-wales-2019-to-2020/hate-crime-england-and-wales-2019-to-2020>

[16]House of Commons: Home Affairs Committee, (2017), 'Hate crime: abuse, hate and extremism online'.
<https://publications.parliament.uk/pa/cm201617/cmselect/cmhaff/609/60902.htm>

[17](Marcus Christenson, 2021) 'Thierry Henry quits social media until companies act on racism and bullying' - The Guardian 26 March 2021

[18]Department for Digital, Culture, Media and Sport, (2019), 'Rapid Evidence Assessment: The Prevalence and Impact of Online Trolling'
<https://assets.publishing.service.gov.uk/government/uploads/system/uploads/attachment_data/file/973971/DCMS_REA_Online_trolling

Football in particular has been rife with cyber hate speech. Just recently in August 2021 it was reported that since her identity leaked, the girlfriend of the footballer Jack Grealish has been receiving 200 death threats a day. She later came out and stated about how the social media platform is toxic[19].

We must now ask ourselves, is online hate crime really just online? The Commission on Race and Ethnic Disparities[20] argues that the visibility of online hate speech, and in particular online racism, misinforms the public about the views of wider society. The Commission claims that it causes society to believe that racism in the UK is more widespread than it actually is. They also say that it causes the importation of divisive and factually incorrect terms from America such as "white privilege".

A more extreme example of online hate crime bleeding out into the real world is the recent attack in August 2021 by Jake Davison. Davison had previously posted videos on YouTube ranting about his hatred towards women, he later murdered five people and then shot himself. After this attack he was praised by 10,000 people within the 'incel' community[21]. This was not an isolated incident or even something new. Even as far back as 2014 in America

_V2.pdf>

[19](Emma Brazell, 2021) 'Jack Grealish's girlfriend bombarded with 200 death threats a day during Euros' - The Metro, 3 August 2021

[20]Commission on Race and Ethnic Disparities: The Report (March 2021)
<https://assets.publishing.service.gov.uk/government/uploads/system/uploads/attachment_data/file/974507/20210331_-_CRED_Report_-_FINAL_-_Web_Accessible.pdf>

[21](Tony Whitfield, 2021) 'Killing Spree a Terror Attack'- Sunday Express, 15 August 2021

such incidents are recorded. In May 2014, another member of the 'incel' community named Elliot Rodgers shot and killed six people after uploading a video to YouTube filled with hate towards women titled "Elliot Rodgers Retribution"[22]. The incident featuring Davison has made the public wonder why the police did not conduct an extensive social media check on Davison before he was issued a gun licence and furthermore why tech companies failed to remove Davison's hate speech messages.

Online hate speech can also have a real-world impact by influencing disenfranchised schoolchildren. After the Columbine shooting of 1999, an online cult began, known as 'Columbiners', who aim to lure in and inspire other schoolchildren to commit mass school shootings as well as spread hate[23]. Multiple school shooters in recent years have publicly stated their devotion to the Columbine shooters online[24]. This is still ongoing today, it was reported that after the gunman Nikolas Cruz committed the 2018 Parkland shooting, he received 'a sack of fan mail' as well as racy photos from female admirers[25].

A Discussion of Legislative Framework to Explain How Cyber Hate Crime Offences Are Regulated

An academic has suggested that there are two reasons why hate speech should be regulated[26]. One reason is because it

---

[22](Elliot Rodger, 2014) "Elliot Rodger manifesto outlines plans for Santa Barbara attack". The Sydney Morning Herald, May 25 2014

[23](Johann Hari, 2004) 'The cult of Eric and Dylan' - The Independent, 15 February 2004

[24](Associated Press, 2016) 'Columbine killer has cult of fans long after death' - New York Post, 24 February 2016

[25](Jimmy McClosky, 2018) 'Florida school shooter Nikolas Cruz gets sent sackfuls of fan mail and sexy photos' - The Metro, 29 March 2018

is likely to transpire into the 'real world' and eventually result in the actual harm of a targeted group. The other reason is because it undermines the status of the targeted person as a free and equal member of society.

There are many regulations inside the UK against online hate crime. The Crime and Disorder Act (1998)[27] prohibits a number of offences which include racially aggravated crime based on offences such as assault, harassment and abusive behaviour. Furthermore Section 145 of the Criminal Justice Act (2003)[28] calls upon the courts to increase the sentence of any offence that involves the perpetrator showing the victim hostility based upon his protected characteristics or the offence being in some way motivated by the victims protected characteristics such as race, religion or disability. The UK government has also regulated racist chanting at football matches and inciting hatred based on protected characteristics[29].

Over the years, case law in the UK has further regulated and backed up laws on both real world and online hate crime. Case law has stated that the definition of a racial group encompasses more than just ethnic origin and also includes nationality[30]. Case law also clarified that it does not matter if someone has multiple reasons for uttering racial abuse, it is not acceptable[31]. In fact, even if the

---

[26](O'Regan, 2018) 'Hate speech regulation on social media: An intractable contemporary challenge'

[27]Crime and Disorder Act (1998)

[28]Criminal Justice Act (2003)

[29](United kingdom (England and Wales): Responding to Hate Speech, 2018) <https://www.article19.org/wp-content/uploads/2018/06/UK-hate-speech_March-2018.pdf>

[30]R v Rogers (2007) 2 W.L.R. 280

defendant is not bothered by the remark, the use of racist abuse during an offence is enough to pass the test for racial aggravation[32].

In regards to hate crime and cyber hate crime, when an offence is committed, prosecutors must cautiously decide whether or not it is in the public interest to charge certain offenders. This is because there are certain factors that should be taken into account. The main reason is because people in a free and democratic society have the right to voice their opinions even if these opinions may cause offence to some, the freedom of expression guaranteed to us must be balanced with the states duty to protect the public's safety. Furthermore, Section 29J of the Racial and Religious Hatred Act 2006 confirms that, despite the acts creation of many hate offences, the act does not prohibit a person from enacting criticism, insult or dislike of a certain religion or its adherents[33].

In the European Union, measures have also been taken to regulate cyber hate crimes. Though article 10 of the European Convention on Human Rights grants all people the right to freedom of expression[34], it is specifically stated in Article 17 of the European Convention on Human Rights that nothing in the convention can be interpreted in a way which allows any state, group or person to "engage in any activity or perform any act aimed at the destruction of any
of the rights and freedoms set forth" in the convention. This means that while the European Union recognises the

---

[31]DPP v McFarlane (2002) EWHC 485 (Admin),

[32]R v Woods (2002) EWHC 85

[33]Racial and Religious Hatred Act (2006)

[34]European Convention on Human Rights - Article 10

right to freedom of expression, it denies anyone the right to attempt to use the European Convention of Human rights to attempt to destroy another person's rights, such as is common through online hate speech. Furthermore, the European Unions 'Additional Protocol to the Convention on Cybercrime, concerning the criminalisation of acts of a racist and xenophobic nature committed through computer systems' requires that participating states outlaw the distribution of xenophobic and racist materials through the internet as well as the denial of genocide[35].

In international law, there have also been measures put in place to protect people from cyber hate crimes. Article 20 of the International Covenant on Civil and Political Rights requires that nations outlaw "any advocacy of national, racial, or religious hatred that constitutes incitement to discrimination, hostility, or violence"[36]. Recently, the United Nations Human Rights Council also stated that the rights that people have offline should also be protected online, this includes the right to be free of discrimination[37].

A Discussion of Law Enforcement Challenges and the Impact of the COVID-19 Pandemic

One problem that lawmakers have is that they have an onus to balance the right to free speech against the wellbeing of society. Article 10 of the Human Rights Act[38]

---

[35] Additional Protocol to the Convention on Cybercrime, concerning the criminalisation of acts of a racist and xenophobic nature committed through computer systems' (ETS No. 189)

[36] International Covenant on Civil and Political Rights - Article 20

[37] HRC 38th 04/07/2018 A/HRC/38/L.10/Rev.1 The promotion, protection and enjoyment of human rights on the Internet.

gives everyone the right to freedom of expression. This commonly leads to those who are convicted of hate speech arguing that they merely expressing their right to freedom of expression. In the case of Redmond-Bate v DPP[39] it was stated that freedom of speech means nothing if it does not include the freedom to be irritating, unwelcome and provocative so long as it does not provoke violence. Furthermore, in the case of Chambers v DPP[40] The judge ruled that the defendant lacked a mens rea because "he intended the message as a joke". This shows that there is a difficulty for law enforcement to secure a successful conviction because there is a difficulty in balancing freedom of speech against a society's wellbeing.

Academics have pointed out a few other challenges that could affect law enforcement in regards to regulating hate speech[41]. One of these challenges is that there is no clear definition as to how the words 'hateful', 'discriminatory' and 'degrading' should be defined as well as who should be given the responsibility of defining the words in question. Another issue that academics have pointed out is that hate speech laws vary from country to country[42] and because there is no single universal definition it makes it tougher to prosecute those who commit hate speech crimes abroad.

The advancement of online technology also allows for the anonymous sending of messages. This makes it harder for law enforcement to identify the real-world people behind

---

[38]Human Rights Act (1998)

[39]Redmond-Bate v Director of Public Prosecutions (1999) EWHC Admin 733

[40]Chambers v Director for Public Prosecutions (2021) EWHC 2157

[41]Yar M. (2013) 'Cybercrime and Society'

[42]Yar M. (2013) 'Cybercrime and Society'

the accounts spewing hate speech. Tech companies have not made it easy to identify the culprits. It was reported in November 2021 that in the US, the Los Angeles Police Department were making fake Facebook accounts in order to spy on those who are suspected of committing crimes both online and offline. However, Facebook have identified and shut down the police accounts and told the Los Angeles Police Department that what they are doing breaches Facebook's terms of service and to stop[43].

Studies show that the COVID-19 pandemic has led to an increase of hate crime against people of Asian origin and especially against those of Chinese origin[44]. 'Ditch the Label' recently released a report that stated that during the covid pandemic, online hate speech has risen by 20%[45]. The report further shows that in the UK, 27% of all analysed hate speech examples include some form of violent threats.

A Discussion of Suggested Solutions to Identified Law Enforcement Challenges

In October 2021, Frances Haugen, a former Facebook employee, testified before congress to say that Facebook has been misleading the public on its progress against hate speech. She has claimed that Facebook put profits before public safety[46]. She also called on the government to

---

[43](Mary-Ann Russon, 2021) 'Facebook tells LA police to stop spying on users with fake accounts' - BBC News, 19 November 2021

[44]Gray, C. and Hansen, K., 2021. Did Covid-19 Lead to an Increase in Hate Crimes Toward Chinese People in London? Journal of Contemporary Criminal Justice, 37(4), pp.569-588.

[45]Brandwatch. 2021. Uncovered: Online Hate Speech in the Covid Era. <https://www.brandwatch.com/reports/online-hate-speech/view/>

[46](Billy Perrigo, 2021) 'Inside Frances Haugen's Decision to Take on

regulate Facebook and other large tech companies.

The Commission on Race and Ethnic Disparities has recently called for the Government to use Online Safety legislation to address online hate speech, including anonymous hate speech[47]. It also called for social media companies to do more to prevent online hate speech. They furthermore called upon the government to "name and shame" companies which fail to act.

Furthermore, in May 2021, the Online Harm Bill was included in the Queen's Speech. The Online Harm Bills intention is to provide a rigid framework to establish what constitutes harmful content and cyber hate speech among other things. The bill is also supposed to make sure that tech companies are held accountable for their role in the promotion of online hate speech.

Another potential solution to remove online hate speech that is being tested by tech companies currently is to use an Ai system to remove sites which spew hate speech. However, this has backfired as it has been found that some websites that campaign against online hate speech have used real examples of online hate speech that include words such as "nigger" and "nazi" and have then afterwards had their website removed by the Ai systems for alleged racism[48].

Facebook' - TIME, 22 November 2021

[47]Commission on Race and Ethnic Disparities: The Report (March 2021)
<https://assets.publishing.service.gov.uk/government/uploads/system/uploads/attachment_data/file/974507/20210331_-_CRED_Report_-_FINAL_-_Web_Accessible.pdf>

[48]Xindex, (2019), 'Index on Censorship submission to Online Harms White Paper consultation'

Conclusion

In my opinion, online hate speech is posing a bigger problem by the day and it is very clear why this is. In my opinion, it is clear that this is because big tech companies are not doing enough. Public figures, footballers in particular, have constantly called for tech companies to do more to battle online hate speech. These calls are echoed by various commissions on hate which shows that there is a clear need for tech companies to act further. We can only wait and see if the new Online Harms Bill will be an effective method that is efficient in forcing tech companies to do more.

2 THE LIBERIAN CIVIL WARS: WAS THERE A BREACH OF INTERNATIONAL HUMAN RIGHTS STANDARD IN RELATION TO THE RIGHTS OF CHILDREN AND ETHNIC GENOCIDE?

Introduction

In this paper, I will set out to answer the question of whether or not there was a breach of the international human rights standard in regards to ethnic genocide and the rights of children. I will begin my essay by giving a very brief backstory on the country of Liberia. I will then discuss the Genocide during the civil war period as well as the national Liberian position and response as well as the international position. I will then do the same for the use of child soldiers. Following this, I will discuss why some high-profile war criminals have not been prosecuted. I will finally end with a conclusion as well as give my opinion on some practical solutions.

A Brief Backstory

For just over a century, Liberia was ruled by freed slaves known as 'Americo-Liberians', however, in 1980 a native from the Krahn ethnic group known as Samuel Doe took power. In 1989 an Americo-Liberian known as Charles Taylor commenced a coup and the first civil war began which lasted until 1997 and ended with Charles Taylor taking power. However, peace did not last long as tensions continued and another civil war began which lasted from 1999 until 2003 which ended with Charles Taylor being arrested and sentenced at The Hague.

Genocide During the Civil Wars

During the civil wars, genocide was committed by both pro-government and anti-government forces. According to the researcher Stephen Ellis, it was estimated that during 1990 alone, roughly 25,000 people were killed with many of them being civilians who were suspected to be assisting the opposing forces due to their ethnic groups[49]. Despite the Economic Community of West African States (ECOWAS) sending a peacekeeping force in 1990, the genocides continued. During the civil wars, Africa Watch interviewed a number of refugees to gather their accounts and they all tell similar harrowing tales. One refugee gave an account which shows us just how tied in ethnic genocide was to the civil wars, "They (the rebels) killed everybody in the area -- Krahn, Mandingo, and Bassa. They didn't try to choose between the groups, but killed everybody because they thought they were all Krahn in Grand Gedeh"[50]. Africa Watch gave a similar account in their report, this time about genocide committed by government forces. In their 1990 report they describe the atrocities committed by the Liberian army in its counterinsurgency campaign. Abuses included indiscriminate killing of men, women, and children. Civilians were killed merely on the suspicion that they were of the Mano or the Gio ethnicity[51]. These abuses are a

---

[49]Ellis, Stephen. "Liberia 1989-1994: A study of ethnic and spiritual violence." African Affairs 94, issue no. 375 (1995).

[50]Africa Watch, Interview in Pahoubli, September 16 1990.

[51]Africa Watch, "Liberia: A Human Rights Disaster", (1990).

clear and direct disrespect of international human rights law as they breach the Geneva Convention Article 3 which states "Persons taking no active part in the hostilities … shall in all circumstances be treated humanely, without any adverse distinction founded on race, colour, religion or faith, sex, birth or wealth, or any other similar criteria"[52].

The national position of Liberia in regards to genocide is quite clear. Whilst Section 13 of the Liberian Penal Code 1976[53] prohibits discrimination, there have never been any direct Liberian national laws prohibiting genocide. The country of Liberia is however a signatory of the Geneva Convention as well as a signatory to the Convention on the Prevention and Punishment of the Crime of Genocide. Though it is important to note that in recent times, The Truth and Reconciliation Commission's review of genocide during the civil wars has described the enhancement of Liberia's international commitments to prevent genocide while upholding legal architecture as a "complicated task"[54].

It is also incredibly reasonable to believe that the genocide during the civil wars was not merely committed by rogue soldiers or groups, due to how widespread it was. Furthermore, those in top positions during the civil wars failed to act upon hearing about the genocide committed by their troops. During the civil wars, Africa Watch reported that they were particularly concerned about the failure by Charles Taylor to take any measures to prevent indiscriminate killings based on ethnicity. Further

---

[52]International Committee of the Red Cross (ICRC), Geneva Convention Relative to the Treatment of Prisoners of War (Third Geneva Convention), (1949), 75 UNTS 135.

[53]Liberian Penal Code (1976)

[54]Truth and Reconciliation Commission Final Report (Volume ii) (2009)

interviews that took place during the war described bodies being lined across roads and soldiers bragging how many Krahns they killed today. One interview described rebel forces killing everyone in a village who could not speak Mano or Gio[55]. On top of this, in some instances those who were in high-ranking positions participated in the genocide. After the death of Samuel Doe, the government forces were led by General Nimley who decided to set up a so called "death squad" which decided to continue committing ethnic genocide as well as began to kill homeless people and the mentally unwell for fun, supposedly with their leader's approval[56].

Attempts to prevent the genocide were also unwelcomed by the parties during the civil wars. According to the 1990 Africa Watch report, a colonel in the government forces known as Col. Chris Doe tried to limit human rights abuses including genocide committed by his soldiers and was imprisoned as a result[57]. From these findings, we can gather that there was a clear breach of international human rights standard in relation to ethnic genocide during the civil wars from all sides with no major players in the wars attempting to reduce them and those soldiers who found themselves in moral disagreement with it, being arrested.

Child Soldiers During the Civil Wars

During the civil wars, child soldiers were used by both pro-government and rebel forces. A study by Child Soldiers International estimates that between 15,000-

---

[55] Africa Watch, Interview in Abidjan, September 13, 1990.

[56] BBC World Service, "Reporters Visit Monrovia's Airport Killing Field," October 10, 1990.

[57] Africa Watch, "Liberia: A Human Rights Disaster", (1990).

20,000 child soldiers fought in the Liberian civil wars. They also recognise that both pro-government forces and rebel forces used incredibly large amounts of child soldiers[58]. Interviews with witnesses describe soldiers coercing children into fighting with the promise of revenge for the death of their loved ones[59]. Another interview contained two nurses describing children fighting for the rebels who appeared as young as 7 years old with guns that are bigger than they are[60]. The use of child soldiers were not occasional cases of children who were 15, who claimed to be older. There was direct knowledge by all parties that they were enlisting children. A Study report funded by the Ministry of Japan in 2001 discovered that of 4,306 child soldiers in the Liberian civil wars (20% of the total number of fighters demobilised) the majority 69% were as young as 10 or 12 when they joined[61]. Of course, this is a direct breach of Additional Protocol 2 of the Geneva Convention which clearly states that children under the age of 15 should not be recruited or conscripted into armed forces or groups and should also not be permitted to take part in hostilities[62].

The use of child soldiers during the Liberian civil wars was encouraged heavily by all parties to bolster their armies. Charles Taylor's National Patriotic Front of Liberia had military units filled almost exclusively with child soldiers

[58]Child Soldiers International, "Child Soldiers Global Report 2001 - Liberia", (2001).

[59]Africa Watch, Interview in Tabou City, September 14, 1990.

[60]Africa Watch, Interview, September 17, 1990.

[61]Deng, William Deng. "A Survey of Programs on the Reintegration of Former Child Soldiers: Country Profile: Liberia", (2001).

[62]Protocol Additional to the Geneva Conventions of 12 August 1949, and relating to the Protection of Victims of Non-International Armed Conflicts (Protocol II), 1125 UNTS 609

known as Small Boys Units in 1990 and repeated these actions during the war in Sierra Leone[63]. Observers from Human Rights Watch described the siege of Monrovia that occurred during the Liberian civil wars as chaotic and filled with many very young fighters shooting weapons which they had not been trained to use[64].

Liberia possesses no national laws against the use of child soldiers and the Liberian Constitution makes no mention of minimum age for children to fight in hostilities[65]. However, in the year 2000, the UN General Assembly adopted the Optional Protocol to the Convention on the Rights of the Child on the involvement of children in armed conflict to protect children from recruitment and use in hostilities which was signed by Liberia. The government of Liberia during the civil wars have (despite evidence to the contrary) constantly denied that they were using child soldiers. In 1999, Liberian authorities vehemently denied that any abuse or recruitment of children by the Armed Forces of Liberia were taking place[66].

It is also important to note that the child soldiers were grossly mistreated before battle. One former warlord known as Joshua Blahyi appeared on a documentary where he claimed that he used to force child soldiers to take large doses of cocaine to make them more effective in combat[67].

---

[63]Barrowclough, Erin. "U.S Court Convicts Charles Taylor's Son of Torture" The Times Online, 7 December 2010

[64]Human Rights Watch, LIBERIA Waging War to Keep the Peace: The ECOMOG Intervention and Human Rights, June 1993

[65]Constitution of Liberia (1986)

[66]African Conference on the Use of Child Soldiers, Maputo, Mozambique, 19 to 22 April 1999.

[67]The Vice Guide To Liberia (2010)

A report by Human Rights Watch recognises that many child soldiers were forced to rape, torture and kill other people in order to instil loyalty[68]. From these findings, we can gather that there was a clear breach of international human rights standards in relation to the rights of children during the Liberian civil wars from all sides with children being forced and coerced into fighting and committing war crimes as well as being treated extremely poorly by those in charge.

Lack of Prosecutions

After the second civil war had ended, almost everyone who were guilty of committing war crimes were allowed to continue on with their lives. In 2005, the government of Liberia set up the Liberian Truth and Reconciliation Commission in order to investigate all of the human rights atrocities that occurred during the Liberian civil wars. However, following its final report, the Liberian Truth and Reconciliation Commission were been strongly criticised by Amnesty International due to its lack of legal powers[69]. According to the Liberian Truth and Reconciliation Commission's final report, over 50,000 human rights violations were committed during the civil war period with evidence of at least 28,042 murders[70]. This raises a question, why haven't there been widespread prosecutions of those responsible for the atrocities committed during the Liberian civil wars.

We must ask why more hasn't been done to prosecute war

---

[68]Human Rights Watch, "Easy Prey: Child Soldiers in Liberia", (1994)

[69]Aning, Kwesi, and Thomas Jaye. "Liberia: A briefing paper on the TRC report." Occasional Paper 33, (2011)

[70]Truth and Reconciliation Commission Final Report (Volume ii)

criminals by the Liberian national government. The first issue arises when we recognise that the Liberian Truth and Reconciliation Commission (who were set up to handle this) had no legal authority within Liberia. This has led to a complete lack of prosecutions within the Liberian judiciary system, with failure to prosecute even a single person for atrocities committed during the civil wars[71]. One culprit who stood in front of the Liberian Truth and Reconciliation Commission in 2008 was Joshua Blahyi. Despite Blahyi's testimony that he used child soldiers and killed up to 20,000 people, he was allowed to walk free[72]. Blahyi has publicly called for a war crimes court to be established in Liberia so that he and others perpetrators can account for the crimes they have committed[73].

This raises yet another question. Why do the Liberian government not give more power to the Liberian Truth and Reconciliation Commission? One man who committed several acts of ethnic genocide and has used child soldiers was a former warlord known as Prince Johnson. There are recorded incidences of Prince Johnson murdering foreign aid workers in full view of the international press and committing other atrocities[74]. Despite being one of the more infamous examples, he has yet to face any prosecution. In 2005 Prince Johnson won a seat in the Liberian senate and has allegedly voted against any justice being given to the victims of genocide during

---

[71]Human Rights Watch, Justice for Civil Wars-Era Crimes in Liberia, (2019).

[72]Truth and Reconciliation Commission Final Report (Volume ii)

[73]Johnson, Obediah (June 3, 2021). "Liberia: Ex-warlord "General Butt Naked" Wants Sen. Prince Johnson, Others, Tell Their Stories at War Crimes Court". FrontPage Africa.

[74]"Marines Evacuate 21 More in Liberia," New York Times, August 8, 1990.

the Liberian civil war and even ran for presidency of Liberia in 2011[75]. In 2009, the Liberian Truth and Reconciliation Commission recommended that Prince Johnson be barred from politics and his response was to issue a harrowing response and claim that if the Liberian government go forward with the decision, then he will mobilise his former army[76]. Furthermore, the former president of Liberia (Ellen-Johnson Sirleaf) was also recommended to be barred from politics by the Liberian Truth and Reconciliation Commission but was still able to hold the position of president. This infiltration by war criminals into the Liberian government has led to an inability for effective justice to be received. The Liberian lawyer Charles Sunwabe gives a clear and simple explanation as to why legal action has not been taken: "This noble quest for justice is being resisted by some biased Liberian politicians"[77]. This comment is echoed by the Executive Director of the Liberia Peacebuilding Office, Edward Mulbah, who states that "Those who enjoy state power are not keen about evaluating their role in the war"[78].

Despite the influence of former warlords within the Liberian political system, calls remain for the establishment of a war crimes court within Liberia. One former child soldier, Arthur Bondo, said in an interview that if a war

---

[75]African Arguments, "You have to face justice so I can get peace": Calls for war court in Liberia, Lucinda Rouse, February 14, 2019

[76]African Arguments, "You have to face justice so I can get peace": Calls for war court in Liberia, Lucinda Rouse, February 14, 2019

[77]Sunwabe, Charles, "We the Victims: Why Liberians Must Demand a War Crimes Tribunal For the Prosecution of Crimes Against Humanity", The Perspective, January 25, 2013.

[78]African Arguments, "You have to face justice so I can get peace": Calls for war court in Liberia, Lucinda Rouse, February 14, 2019

crimes court is finally brought to Liberia, then child soldiers wouldn't be used again[79]. Adama Dempster, who is a campaigner for the Civil Society Human Rights Advocacy Platform of Liberia has constantly called for a war crimes court and stated that it would finally give "victims an opportunity for legal redress"[80]. He has further stated that he believes that the failure to address the human right violations of the past has led to an undermining of present human rights within Liberia[81]. Unfortunately, even now, the calls from human rights campaigners go unheard by those in power in Liberia. In 2019, president Weah responded to the calls for a war crimes court to be established and said "Why now? When we have economic issues, why focus on a war crimes court now?"

However, some prosecutions have taken place abroad. One such prosecution is the incredibly high-profile prosecution of Charles Taylor in 2012[82]. Trials in foreign countries are continuing to this day. In 2020 Gibril Massaquoi was arrested and put on trial in Finland for the crimes that he committed during the Liberian civil wars[83]. This raises an interesting question and potential solution, why is there not some form of a hybrid United Nations court in Liberia to prosecute those guilty of genocide and

---

[79]Dounard, Bondo, "Thousands dead but no prosecutions - why Liberia has not acted", BBC March 1, 2021.

[80]Dounard, Bondo, "Thousands dead but no prosecutions - why Liberia has not acted", BBC March 1, 2021.

[81]Dounard, Bondo, "Thousands dead but no prosecutions - why Liberia has not acted", BBC March 1, 2021.

[82]BBC, Charles Taylor war crimes convictions upheld, BBC, 26 September 2013.

[83]BBC, Liberia war crimes: Sierra Leone rebel commander acquitted by court in Finland, BBC, 29 April, 2020.

other war crimes? This is not an outlandish idea. As we know, a UN-backed Special Court for Sierra Leone was set up in 2002 after the Sierra Leone civil war. This was considered a great success and at the time the UN Secretary-General Ban Ki-moon gave praise to the court for its impressive legacy and role that it had played in advancing the global quest for accountability[84]. The reason that this cannot be replicated in Liberia is because the Special Court for Sierra Leone was established because of an agreement between the United Nations and the Sierra Leonean government. The court was set up by the request of the Sierra Leonean government, not forcefully implemented by the United Nations. To install a hybrid United Nations court in Liberia, it would likely require the request of the Liberian government and because of the perpetrators remaining in positions of political power within Liberia, such an option seems incredibly unlikely. In conclusion, despite many calls from activists, it seems incredibly unlikely that we will be able to see justice for the events of the Liberian civil war until those who have committed ethnic genocide and used child soldiers are removed from the Liberian government. It is evident that justice has not been done as in 2018, the United Nations Human Rights Committee expressed concern over continuing impunity in Liberia for the actions done during the civil wars period and again calling for justice and reparations to take place[85].

Conclusion

In conclusion, we can see that both genocide and the use

---

[84]The Special Court for Sierra Leone rests – for good, Africa Renewal ,April 2014, Lansana Gberie

[85]UN Human Rights Committee, Concluding observations on the initial report of Liberia, 6 July 2018

of child soldiers were both prevalent and obvious during the Liberian civil wars. The international human rights standard was immensely breached. Though countless attempts have been made by many activists and much talk has been done by both international institutions and some figures within the Liberian political system, no prosecutions for the war crimes that took place during the civil war period have taken place within the Liberian legal system. The only trials that have taken place, have taken place in foreign nations. It is evident that those who have committed ethnic genocide and used child soldiers have infiltrated the Liberian political system and made it impossible to prosecute them.

Recommendations

In my opinion, there is a lot more that needs to be done. Of course, establishing a hybrid United Nations war crimes court and dealing with corruption within the Liberian political system are desirable outcomes, however there are many smaller and more realistic recommendations that I will recommend.

Firstly, I believe that we should reinforce the international commitment to continue prosecuting warlords in foreign territories. This could lead to the continuation of successful convictions for the ethnic genocide and other crimes that have taken place during the Liberian civil war period.

My other recommendation is that the Liberian government follows the 'Palava Hut' recommendation that was given in the Truth and Reconciliation Commission's final report. The 'Palava Hut' would allow victims to confront perpetrators in a face-to-face setting and allow victims to gather answers to the questions they've always desired as well as explain to the perpetrators how they felt. Whilst it is not ideal when compared to a successful conviction, perhaps with the current political situation in Liberia, this is as much as we can give the victims.

3 THE SECOND AMENDMENT, A POLARIZED OPINION

"A well-regulated Militia, being necessary to the security of a free State, the right of the people to keep and bear Arms, shall not be infringed."[86], these are the words of the second amendment, a cornerstone in the foundation of the United States of America. At the time of the Bill of Rights conception, it was the belief of the founding fathers that citizens should be able to protect themselves against the government and any other threat to their wellbeing or personal freedom[87], which in my opinion was made with the intent of pure heart but can it still remain unchecked in today's era where the technology of weaponry is vastly advancing. In this essay, I will discuss the second amendment's historical background, the advancement of its interpretation overtime and the effect of the recent case, New York State Rifle & Pistol Association, Inc. v. Bruen (2022).

In regards to the historical context of the second amendment, it is crucial to immediately note that it was ratified less than 10 years after the American Revolutionary war. As one journalist puts it, "All 10 amendments" were aimed to prevent a repeat of the "oppressions they (the founding fathers) had suffered under British rule."[88] The

---

[86]https://constitution.congress.gov/constitution/amendment-2/

[87]https://www.nraila.org/what-is-the-second-amendment-and-how-is-it-defined/#:~:text=The%20Founding%20Fathers%20felt%20that,defend%20themselves%20and%20their%20property.

[88]https://www.clarionledger.com/story/opinion/columnists/2017/10/

intent of the founders including the second amendment was to prevent tyranny and give the people a method of fighting back in the event of a tyrannical government. In a letter to James Madison, Thomas Jefferson even wrote "Malo periculosam, libertatem quam quietam servitutem."[89] (roughly translated as "I prefer dangerous freedom over peaceful slavery"). During the revolutionary war, each of the colonies that declared independence from Britain and formed the United States had armed militia units and these were essential to the American victory[90]. Furthermore, it is likely that the founding fathers were heavily influenced by King Georges attempt to disarm the colonies prior to the arrest of patriot political leaders[91]. By tightly holding onto the right to bear arms, it was likely the belief of the founding fathers that the ideal of the constitution would forever remain protected.

Over the course of time, the interpretation of the second amendment has advanced and stroked up many debates and cases that have made their way to the supreme court which still continue to cause controversy in the incredibly polarized America that we see today. Until the late 20th century, there was little scholarly commentary of the

---

09/founding-fathers-created-2nd-amendment-fight-oppressors/746135001/

[89]https://www.monticello.org/research-education/thomas-jefferson-encyclopedia/i-prefer-dangerous-freedom-over-peaceful-slavery-quotation/

[90]Linder, Doug (2008). "United States vs. Miller (U.S. 1939)". Exploring Constitutional Law. University of Missouri-Kansas City Law School. http://www.law.umkc.edu/faculty/projects/ftrials/conlaw/millervus.html

[91]https://www.washingtonpost.com/archive/opinions/1995/05/31/when-the-redcoats-confiscated-guns/e38d0810-af85-4949-8d93-3da746601e65/King George III ordered the seizure of any firearms imported into the colonies.

Second Amendment[92].

One of the first critical cases regarding the second amendment that made it to the United States v Miller (1939)[93]. This case added clarity and addressed where military-style weapons fitted in. Justice McReynolds stated that in regards to the defendant's weaponry did not have any reasonable relation "to the preservation or efficiency of a well-regulated militia, and therefore cannot say that the Second Amendment guarantees to the citizen the right to keep and bear such a weapon."[94] By using this ruling, it is clear that the court held that the appointed second amendment rights have an affixation to the preservation of a well-regulated militia. Therefore, it is rational to expect that weaponry not matching this criteria could have some restrictions.

Another case that it is imperative to mention is the District of Columbia v Heller (2008)[95]. This case is widely regarded by scholars to have had a major effect on the interpretation of the second amendment. This is because it was the first occasion where the Supreme Court affirmed that an individual has the right to own a gun.[96] However it is also crucial to note that Justice Antonin Scalia stated that "the right secured by the Second Amendment is not unlimited".[97] This means that while one has the right to

---

[92]Garry Wills, A Necessary Evil: A History of American Distrust of Government, Simon and Schuster, 1999, p. 252.

[93]United States v. Miller, 307 U.S. 174 (1939)

[94]United States v. Miller, 307 U.S. 174 (1939),

[95]District of Columbia v. Heller, 554 U.S. 570 (2008)

[96]Liptak, Adam (March 16, 2009). "Few Ripples From Supreme Court Ruling on Guns". The New York Times https://www.nytimes.com/2009/03/17/us/17bar.html

bear arms, that right may come with restrictions such as those listed by Justice Antonin Scalia which were "prohibitions on the possession of firearms by felons and the mentally ill, or laws forbidding the carrying of firearms in sensitive places such as schools and government buildings."[98] This case was further reinforced with the latter case of McDonald v City of Chicago (2010)[99] where the purpose of the second amendment was further explained with Justice Alito stating that the decision made in District of Columbia v Heller (2008) protects "the right to possess a handgun in the house for the purposes of self-defense."[100]

When it comes to the interpretation of the second amendment, there are two major perspectives. The first interpretation is the collective right interpretation (also known as the states' rights approach) which argued that the Second Amendment is not applicable to the individual person but rather, it recognizes the right of each individual state to arm a militia. Some scholars argue in favor of this point with one stating that citizens "have no right to keep or bear arms, but the states have a collective right to have the National Guard".[101] The second interpretation is the

---

[97]Robert A. Sedler (June 30, 2008). "Ruling upholds most gun control laws". The Detroit News.
http://m.detnews.com/detail.jsp?key=279156&full=1

[98]Robert A. Sedler (June 30, 2008). "Ruling upholds most gun control laws". The Detroit News.
http://m.detnews.com/detail.jsp?key=279156&full=1

[99]McDonald v. City of Chicago, 561 U.S. 742 (2010)

[100]Picadio, Anthony P. (January 2019). "The Right to Bear Arms a Disfavored Right". Pennsylvania Bar Association Quarterly
https://www.documentcloud.org/documents/5732643-The-Right-to-Bear-Arms-a-Disfavored-Right.html

[101]Halbrook, Stephen P. (1998). Freedmen, the 14th Amendment, and

individual rights interpretation (also known as the standard model) which argues that the particular language used within the second amendment confers a right to every individual to keep and bear arms. However, this debate between interpretations was effectively quashed when the previously mentioned cases reached their resolution and conferred some individual rights upon citizens.[102]

I will now discuss the recent case of New York State Rifle & Pistol Association, Inc. v Bruen (2022)[103]. In regards to this case, the specific point that was honed in on is the question of "whether the State's denial of petitioners' applications for concealed-carry licenses for self-defense violated the Second Amendment"[104] In the ruling, it was held that it was unconstitutional to issue a "may-issue" regulation in regards to firearms and that furthermore, the right to public possession of a firearm is deeply protected under the second amendment. So far, this outcome has had a major impact on the effects of the second amendment and more particularly, on challenges towards its regulation. Once the outcome had been decided, many began to suspect that "may-issue" firearm regulations would begin to be amended or challenged across the United States[105]. Shortly after the resolution, many states

---

the Right to Bear Arms, 1866–1876. Greenwood Publishing Group.

[102]"How the NRA rewrote the Second Amendment". Brennan Center for Justice. https://www.brennancenter.org/our-work/research-reports/how-nra-rewrote-second-amendment

[103]New York State Rifle & Pistol Association, Inc. v. Bruen, 142 S.Ct. 2111 (2022)

[104]Millhiser, Ian (April 26, 2021). "The Supreme Court will hear a major Second Amendment case that could gut US gun laws" https://www.vox.com/2021/4/26/22364154/supreme-court-guns-second-amendment-new-york-state-rifle-corlett-shootings-kavanaugh-barrett

began to amend their laws including California, New Jersey and Hawaii[106].Furthermore, multiple legal challenges have been brought against different states since then, relaxing the restrictions on who can own guns in certain states[107]. This is likely a trend that will continue with NRA president Dudley Brown stating that the decision is a "bulwark against regulation" and that it would help the NRA "win a host of lawsuits against gun restrictions"[108].

There are two massively polarized viewpoints on whether or not there should be more restrictions on gun ownerships. For example, one side argues that more gun control laws would reduce gun deaths whilst the other argues that gun ownership deters crime. One specific example I would like to cover is the opposing viewpoints in regards to high powered magazines and assault weapons. The gun-control advocates would argue that there should be a much stricter regulation or even outright ban on high powered magazines and assault weapons. This topic first came to light after the Las Vegas gunman

[105]MacDermitt, Jennifer (June 24, 2022). "States brace for fight over gun laws after high court ruling". Associated Press. https://apnews.com/article/us-supreme-court-new-york-jersey-gun-politics-government-and-24a6a82ea365212ecaa7af71f9c72561

[106]"Public Carry Licensing Under Hawaii Law Following New York State Rifle & Pistol Association v. Bruen" (PDF). Ag.hawaii.gov. https://ag.hawaii.gov/wp-content/uploads/2022/07/Attorney-General-Opinion-22-02.pdf

[107]Richer, Alanna Durkin; Whitehurst, Lindsay (February 18, 2023). "Turmoil in courts on gun laws in wake of justices' ruling". Associated Press. https://apnews.com/article/politics-mississippi-state-government-delaware-california-massachusetts-3983cecfd1107c263d5309ec0d80a966

[108] Dewan, Shaila (May 24, 2023). "In Capitols and Courthouses, No End to National Divide Over Gun Policy". The New York Times. https://www.nytimes.com/2023/05/24/us/gun-control-laws-uvalde.html

Stephen Paddock used high powered magazines and assault rifles to commit a massacre from his hotel room[109]. The argument to ban high powered magazines and assault weapons is backed up by the statistics an investigation found that stated that high-capacity magazines were used in at least 50% of mass shootings between the years 1982 and 2012[110]. The need for these high-powered magazines and assault weapons to be banned or regulated is apparently a widely held viewpoint as a poll conducted in 2019 shows that 65% of Americans believed that a ban on high powered magazines in particular would reduce gun violence[111]. However, the opposing viewpoint believes that gun control laws, including those that try to ban assault weapons or high-powered magazines infringe upon the right to own guns for hunting and sport. The National Shooting Sports Foundation, stated in a report that they believe weapons "So-called assault weapons are more often than not less powerful than other hunting rifles." and they believe that "The term 'assault weapon' was conjured up by anti-gun legislators to scare voters into thinking these firearms are something out of a horror movie."[112]

---

[109]High-capacity magazine used by Vegas shooter in high demand By Kevin Dugan (October 4, 2017) https://nypost.com/2017/10/04/high-capacity-magazine-used-by-vegas-shooter-in-high-demand/

[110]Mark Follman and Gavin Aronsen, "'A Killing Machine': Half of All Mass Shooters Used High-Capacity Magazines," Jan. 30, 2013 https://www.motherjones.com/politics/2013/01/high-capacity-magazines-mass-shootings/

[111]Domenico Montanaro, "Americans Largely Support Gun Restrictions to 'Do Something' about Gun Violence," npr.org, Aug. 10, 2019 https://www.npr.org/2019/08/10/749792493/americans-largely-support-gun-restrictions-to-do-something-about-gun-violence

[112]National Shooting Sports Foundation, "Background Information on So-Called 'Assault-Weapons,'" 2011 https://www.nssf.org/wp-

In conclusion, the second amendment is an ever-evolving concept that is continually changing with the times, especially in recent periods where politics in America is so polarized with one side gunning to keep their weapons while the other attempts to push for tighter regulations. I have no doubt that in the future, the interpretations will be either further relaxed or tightened with one side left feeling unhappy. Only time will tell what side of the political debate will have their views enshrined in regards to the gun ownership policy of America

---

content/uploads/2021/05/NSSF-factsheet-Assault-Weaspons.pdf

4 LAW AND DEVELOPMENT IN THE KOREAN PENINSULA: CAN THE NORTH AND SOUTH REACH LEGAL COMPROMISES?

Introduction

The division of the Korean Peninsula into two spheres of influence has been an idea that has been discussed for many hundreds of years. During the 16th century, whilst his invasion of Korea was continuing, Toyotomi Hideyoshi unsuccessfully proposed to the Ming Dynasty that Korea should be split into two spheres of influence[113]. However, the actual division of the Korean Peninsula into South and North Korea actually began after the end of the second world war. Political tensions about the communist sphere of influence began to arise in the western world. After the second world war had ended, Soviet troops began to head towards Korea and the Americans had begun to worry that they would occupy all of Korea. In attempt to prevent this, some American soldiers created a map with a divining line along the 38th parallel of Korea, which the Soviets agreed to[114]. Soviet troops moved into North Korea and American troops moved into South Korea, thus dividing Korea into two spheres of influence. They originally agreed that Korea would be liberated and placed under an international trusteeship until the Korean

[113]Swope, Kenneth. "Beyond Turtleboats: Siege Accounts from Hideyoshi's Second Invasion of Korea, 1597–1598" Sungkyun Journal of East Asian Studies

[114]Oberdorfer, Don; Carlin, Robert (2014). The Two Koreas: A Contemporary History. Basic Books

Peninsula is determined to be able to self-rule under a single government[115]. However, this did not occur, and up to this day, Korea remains divided. In the present day, with North Korea's ties to China and South Korea's ties to Japan and the western world, maybe Hideyoshi posthumously had his goals achieved.

The creation of Korean law and its developments play an arguably large role within the relationship between North Korea and South Korea. Inside the Korean peninsula, the respective countries' laws are more than just a framework to decide what is right and wrong but they act as a baseline for decisions related to the governments, foreign policy and attitudes between the Koreas. The development of the laws of either country is largely also influenced by these factors and factors such as ideologies and political values.

In this essay I will be discussing the legal differences between North Korea and South Korea. As well as this, I will discuss whether or not legal compromises can be made and possibly even a step towards unification (in regards to the countries respective laws) can be made by the Korean governments.

A Historical Analysis

The history of Korean law is a very complex topic due to the extremely different developments within the legal system in North and South Korea. Therefore, gaining an understanding of the history is essential to understand what challenges are posed in reaching legal compromises between the two Korean countries. Before the Korean Peninsula was divided, the Korean legal system was, like many Asian nations, based on the Confucian system[116].

---

[115]Lee, Jongsoo (2006). The Partition of Korea After World War II: A Global History. New York: Palgrave Macmillan

However, following the end of the second world war and the subsequent Korean division, two distinct legal models arose in the Korean peninsula.

The legal system in North Korea immediately began to develop during the Soviet presence in the country. Due to the influence of Communism, the legal system began to put an emphasis on the state having an authoritarian type of control as well as a strong emphasis on their version of equality and the people as a collective over the rights of the person as an individual[117]. One of the key changes was that under section 6 of The Socialist Constitution of the Democratic People's Republic of Korea created the highest legal power in the land, which came to be known as The Supreme People's Assembly under the constitution of North Korea[118]. As well as this, many laws were enforced to support the North Korean ideology of Juche.

In a stark contrast to this, the South Korean legal system began to develop under the influence of western nations such as America. South Korea developed a legal foundation which consisted of civil law and common law principles. Instead of having a Supreme People's Assembly, South Korea enshrined their basic rights through the development of 'The Provisional Charter of Korea' into 'The Constitution of The Republic of Korea'[119]. Furthermore, the Constitutional Court was created in

---

[116]Altman, Albert A. (1984). "Korea's First Newspaper: The Japanese Chōsen shinpō". The Journal of Asian Studies.

[117]Salmon, Andrew (3 December 2018). "Getting to grips with law and business in high-risk North Korea". Asia Times.

[118]The Socialist Constitution of the Democratic People's Republic of Korea - Section 6

[119]Public Administration and Policy in Korea: Its Evolution and Challenges by Keun Namkoong

order to assist with the protection of the rights of the individual[120].

The continued split of the Korean Peninsula continued to result in the applicable legal systems becoming more and more different. The North Korean system of laws was overseen closely by the ruling government and the Kim dynasty in order to use the laws to serve political purposes and keep a tight control on the country[121]. In a stark contrast to this, the law in South Korea continued to use their judicial and governmental tools to strengthen the rights of the individual as well as continue to strengthen the democratic powers to ensure that there are fair balances and that a situation similar to the one in North Korea, couldn't occur[122].

It is also important to mention that relations between the two Korean nations continued to worsen during the Korean War that took place in the 1950s. Following the war, North Korea continued to centralize its legal system powers within the ruling Workers Party government and thus including the Kim dynasty. Furthermore, they also began to grow rapidly, spurred on by funding from China and the Soviet Union[123]. In contrast to this, South Korea continued to promote democracy and began to get their legal system to line up with the rest of the western world.

[120]The National Assembly of the Republic of Korea (https://www.assembly.go.kr/views/cms/assm/assembly/asshistory/asshistory0101.jsp)

[121]Collins, Robert. Marked for Life: Songbun North Korea's Social Classification System

[122]The History of Korean Constitution in terms of its Spirit: A Study on the Introduction of the April 19 Uprising into the Preamble to the Constitution by Hee Kyung Suh

[123]Armstrong, Charles K. (March 16, 2009). "The Destruction and Reconstruction of North Korea, 1950–1960". The Asia-Pacific Journal.

Furthermore, they also began growth, spurred by funding from the United States through the United Nations Korean Reconstruction Agency[124]. The rapid difference in the development of the legal systems would pose many challenges for future legal compromises between the two nations of the Korean Peninsula.

In the years following the Korean war and up until the 1990's, the two countries continued on their respective paths. North Korea continued to advance a legal system based on the Kim dynasty and holding a socialist character closely[125]. South Korea also continued to embrace legal advancements in a democratic legal system and adopted political policies revolving around capitalism and this caused them to begin to attract foreign investments and a boom in growth[126].

Despite the differences between the two nations, there have been a few rare instances where there have been legal interactions and agreements between the two parties. There were talks held in the 1990's that eventually led to the Agreement on Reconciliation, Non-Aggression, Exchanges and Cooperation and the Joint Declaration of the Denuclearization of the Korean Peninsula being created and signed by both nations. This led to things such as the South and the North deciding to establish and operate a South-North joint Nuclear Control Commission within one month of the effectuation of the joint declaration[127]. However, legal agreements and

---

[124]Lyons, Gene M. (1958). "American Policy and the United Nations' Program for Korean Reconstruction"

[125]"North Korea – A Country Study". Library of Congress Country Studies. 2009.

[126]"South Korea: The Economy". Country Studies. Federal Research Division.

compromises between the countries are an extremely rare event with very few examples.

To conclude this segment of historical analysis, North Korea and South Korea have significant differences in their legal systems. With each country having a unique history following the separation of the Korean Peninsula and both parties having widely differing political structures and legal systems. This means that significant challenges will be posed in creating legal compromises between South Korea and North Korea.

A Comparative Legal Analysis in the Frameworks of the Opposing Nations

With the following comparative legal analysis of the legal systems in North Korea and South Korea, I hope to give you an insight into the differences between the laws of each country and speak about some examples of their respective interactions with international law as well as each other.

One area of difference, in regards to the legal framework, is the difference between the laws regarding the protections of the rights and freedoms of individuals. Due to South Korea's democratic system, there is currently a heavy focus on individual rights. Chapter 2 of The Constitution of South Korea guarantees individuals fundamental rights such as that "individuals may not be punished, placed under preventive restrictions" … "Those detained or arrested must be informed of the reason and of their right to an attorney, and family members must be informed. Warrants must be issued by a judge through due procedures, and accused persons may sue for wrongful

---

[127]"Joint Declaration of the Denuclearization of the Korean Peninsula". U.S. State Department

arrest in certain cases"[128]. Furthermore, the existence of the constitutional court in South Korea arguably continues to allow the protection of these rights that are enshrined within the constitution. Unlike this, the legal system in North Korea currently prioritizes the good of the state over the rights of every individual. The North Korean constitution immediately starts with Chapter 1 stating the political structure of the country and how the decision-making procedures all rest with the state and not the people. Article 3 of Chapter 1 states that Kimilsungism-Kimjongilism is the country's guide for its activities and Article 11 makes the Workers' Party of Korea the lead all and every one of the country's activities[129]. Due to these facts and the lack of human rights enshrined in the constitution, basic human rights such as freedom of expression are heavily limited which makes legal compromises involving human rights between the two nations difficult.

A second area of legal difference is in the law regarding the economy as well as rights to ownership of property. Due to the western world's influence, the South Korean legal system allows land purchases and investments into property for the sake of the development of the economy[130]. Laws have been implemented in areas such as contract, intellectual property and regulations within trade and business in order to promote domestic and international investment[131]. This, again, is a vast contrast from the

---

[128]Constitution of the Republic of Korea - Chapter 2

[129]Constitution of the People's Republic of Korea - Chapter 1

[130]Kyung Don Lee, Eun Nyung Lee and Robert C Young, attorneys at Shin & Kim, "Real Estate in South Korea", The Real Estate Review (2nd Edition), March 2013.

[131]Kyung Don Lee, Eun Nyung Lee and Robert C Young, attorneys at Shin & Kim, "Real Estate in South Korea", The Real Estate Review

approach in the law of North Korea. North Korea's framework of socialism puts a great emphasis on how the state should retain control of the property. Staying true to the concept of communism, private land ownership is limited and seizing the means of production is a necessity[132]. Due to the differences in the economic policies of either country and laws regarding private ownership of commodities such as land, finding a common legal ground and reaching legal compromises in this area is a very difficult task.

It is also important to compare trade agreements between these nations and the world at large. The country of South Korea has instinctively gunned towards the pursuit of international trade, in order to improve the economy and continue the rapid development of South Korea. One such example of this is the Korea-United States Free Trade Agreement which was implemented to encourage heavy trade with America and went as far as to eliminate 95% of tariffs on some goods[133]. Furthermore, South Korea also signed up to the Comprehensive and Progressive Agreement for Trans-Pacific Partnership, which further allowed for strengthened trade with other nations across the globe. These legal agreements perfectly capture the South Korean desire to facilitate trade and absorb influence from the surrounding world, both in regards to the legal framework as well as other aspects. This is once again a drastic contrast to North Korea. Due to the Kim dynasties obsession with nuclear weapons, North Korea has been subjected to several sanctions which restrict the

---

(2nd Edition), March 2013.

[132] Andrei Lankov, 'Owning' a home in North Korea, NK News, May 24, 2016

[133] "Landmark U.S.–Korea Free Trade Agreement Enters Into Force". The National Law Review. McDermott Will & Emery 2013

participation of North Korea in the creation of international trade agreements[134]. This leads to North Korea becoming more isolated and will further increase difficulty in an alignment of trade agreements and cooperation between North Korea and South Korea.

Furthermore, as I touched on earlier, the dramatic difference between North Korea and South Korea, in regards to human rights, is greatly apparent. South Korea heavily upholds human rights. The National Human Rights Commission of Korea was founded in South Korea and seeks to not only uphold human rights standards in South Korea, but also to bring them to North Korea (though unsuccessful so far)[135]. The extremely vast differences between these nations in regards to their human rights aspirations as well as all areas creates countless problems in regards to finding common legal grounds to base a foundation of legal compromises upon.

However, despite this, both North Korea and South Korea have, on numerous occasions, stated their desires to promote cooperation between two nations, with the intent to improve relations and someday reunify[136]. In recent years, there have been some occasions where the legal systems of North Korea and South Korea interact successfully such as the Kaesong Industrial Complex. Such initiatives have been attempted in order to try to close some of the extremely wide gaps between the two legal

---

[134]Lee, Yong Suk (2018). "International isolation and regional inequality: Evidence from sanctions on North Korea," Journal of Urban Economics"

[135]Daniel Corks, 2017 "A Lost Decade for Human Rights in South Korea". KOREA EXPOSÉ

[136]Haas, Benjamin; McCurry, Justin; Smith, David (April 27, 2018). "North and South Korean leaders promise 'lasting peace' for peninsula". The Guardian

systems.

To conclude my comparative analysis, North Korea and South Korea have widely different legal structures and legal systems, such as those I have mentioned above and therefore various challenges will be encountered if the attempt to create a unified legal system is made. However, it is important to continue to attempt to find ways to reconcile these differences in order to promote legal cooperation between the two nations with the goal of peace and potential reunification of the Korean Peninsula.

Case Study Example: The Kaesong Industrial Complex

In order to bring light to this topic, I will speak about a particular example that piqued my interest and shows that there is a possibility for legal compromise between North Korea and South Korea. This particular case displays the challenges of legal compromise but also can give hope for further legal cooperation between the nations.

The example that I would like to talk about is the Kaesong Industrial Complex. In 2004, the Kaesong Industrial Complex finished its development in the hermit state of North Korea. The Kaesong Industrial Complex was a joint venture between North Korea and South Korea which sought to attempt to promote economic relations between the two nations. The Kaesong Industrial Complex allows South Korean companies to utilize North Korean labor within the complex. Due to the differences in North Korean and South Korean business law, they needed to put agreements in place to bridge the differences in law. They put in place the 'four agreements' which includes; an agreement on investment protection for South Korean investors in the project, an agreement on the avoidance of double taxation by both North Korea and South Korea and agreements on clearing and procedures on commercial disputes[137]. The legal differences are also bridged over by the use of the Kaesong Industrial Agreements, which covers communications regarding the site, customs clearance, any forms of quarantine as well as entry and exit[138].

The Kaesong Industrial Complex is currently closed, however, both North Korea and South Korea have discussed their desire to reopen it. It was an interesting example of both parties making legal compromises for the benefit of both Koreas, with both sides agreeing on special regulations and dispute resolution methods as well as how to carefully navigate the issue of sanctions[139]. The Kaesong Industrial Complex's shutdown by North Korea, however, highlighted that such cooperative projects between North Korea and South Korea are vulnerable to political tensions within the Korean Peninsula.

Despite these issues, both sides have continued to make efforts to attempt legal cooperation with the opposing party. One example is when in 2018, North Korea and South Korea agreed on signing the Comprehensive Military Agreement which was created with the aim to reduce tension and promote cooperation. It is interesting because both parties were required to cooperate legally and follow the same set of laws in regards to things such as assisting with landmine clearance as well as dismantling guard posts and removal of weapons from the border[140]. Though the creation has had some difficulties, we can use it as an example that legal cooperation between the nations

[137]Professor Rhee - Lecture on East Asian Law - Waseda University

[138]Professor Rhee - Lecture on East Asian Law - Waseda University

[139]An Oasis of Capitalism, Newsweek, 19 September 2005.

[140]Sukjoon Yoon, The. "North and South Korea's New Military Agreement". The Diplomat.

can be possible and have great success.

These very limited cases reveal some of the troubles and potentials of reaching legal compromises between the nations. Whilst the case of the Kaesong Industrial Complex highlighted the weaknesses of legal cooperation in times of political difficulty, it also proved to be a lesson to show that cooperation of the vastly different legal systems can cooperate.

Conclusion

My analysis of the vastly different legal frameworks of North Korea and South Korea highlight the lack of similarities between them. The wildly different histories and spheres of influences affecting either country has caused two completely different legal systems to emerge with a strong difficulty to find common ground. The North Korean socialist legal system placing an emphasis on state control is a stark contrast from the South Korean legal system which has evolved to place a strong importance on democracy. Reaching a legal compromise is further hampered by North Korea's isolation from many international legal agreements while South Korea has an active participation. The difficulty in reaching legal compromises is further displayed by the past attempts of doing so, such as the Kaesong Industrial Complex. In conclusion there are significant problems that will persist with attempting to reach legal compromises with such wildly different systems. I believe that both parties should continue to promote dialogue and go forth and attempt to reach legal compromises. I believe the first step to doing this is to sit down and speak about reopening the Kaesong Industrial Complex. Hopefully, this will lead to further talks and gradually an era where there can be further compromises with the legal systems of South Korea and North Korea.

5 A COMPARISON OF INTERNET SERVICE PROVIDER OBLIGATIONS FOR NATIONAL SECURITY REASONS - CHINA AND ENGLAND

China has quite a few regulations and laws that specify obligations for internet service providers in regards to assisting the police and other governmental agencies in regards to reasons of national security. The first important one is the National Intelligence Law of the People's Republic of China. The second important piece of legislation is the Cybersecurity Law of the People's Republic of China.

The National Intelligence Law of the People's Republic of China puts an onus on all people (including internet service providers) in China to effectively become agents of the state as it states "everyone is responsible for state security"[141]. Furthermore, there are three key articles of this act that are very important to note. These are articles 7, 10 and 18. Article 7 is arguably the most controversial in China and states "All organizations and citizens shall support, assist, and cooperate with national intelligence efforts in accordance with law, and shall protect national intelligence work secrets they are aware of."[142] Which essentially means that all businesses and Internet Service Providers in China have an obligation to hand over

---

[141] Canadian Security Intelligence Service 2018 "China's intelligence law and the country's future intelligence competitions". Government of Canada.

[142] National Intelligence Law of the People's Republic of China - Article 7

information to Chinese intelligence agencies. Furthermore, article 10 states that "As necessary for their work, national intelligence work institutions are to use the necessary means, tactics, and channels to carry out intelligence efforts, domestically and abroad."[143] Which is seen across the world as dangerous because it means that the law may apply extraterritorially, possibly compelling Chinese businesses operating overseas to hand over data, even when operating in foreign jurisdictions[144].

The Cybersecurity Law of the People's Republic of China requires that internet service providers store specific data within China and that the authorities may, at any moment, check the companies network operations as well as that internet service providers must hand over information whenever requested[145].

With these laws in place, the Chinese governmental agencies possess great powers over the internet service providers based in China under the guise of national security purposes. Such handing over of data to government agencies has been criticized as limiting freedom of speech within China because of the obligations to provide your identity to social network services in China[146].

The Chinese government's approach to strong-arming internet service providers into providing tech support has

[143]National Intelligence Law of the People's Republic of China - Article 10

[144]Girard, Bonnie. "The Real Danger of China's National Intelligence Law". The Diplomat. 2021

[145]Wagner, Jack 2017 "China's Cybersecurity Law: What You Need to Know". The Diplomat.

[146]"中国《网络安全法》草案出炉 恐加强言论管制". BBC 中文网 (in Simplified Chinese). 9 July 2015

both advantages and disadvantages to it. One might argue that doing this allows China to safeguard national security and prevent things such as terrorist attacks and killing sprees before they happen. The ability to have easy access to those who commit cyber offenses, such as making murder threats, I believe would act as a preventative measure to stop such cyber offenses from taking place. However, the Chinese approach can also be seen as having a lack of respect for the right to privacy and a strong potential to be abused by powers for political purposes. It allows authorities to find out who holds a belief that is against the status quo beliefs of the Chinese government and can conduct extensive monitoring on these people, leading to a disproportionate intrusion into some individuals' private lives.

The United Kingdom has a distinct approach to the matter, The current obligations of internet service providers for the purposes of national security are listed under the Investigatory Powers Act. However, it is very important to note that the United Kingdom did attempt to take a stronger approach like the Chinese government's approach and introduced the Data Retention and Investigatory Powers Act, however, it was quickly challenged by many human rights groups[147]. This law required internet service providers in the UK to keep records and track the use of the internet in the UK and allow the police and intelligence agencies to access them at any time, without being authorized or challenged by the judicial system[148]. However, in 2015, a legal challenge against the law was taken to the European high court who agreed that the Data Retention and Investigatory Powers Act was incompatible with the Human Rights Act and the

---

[147] "Emergency phone and internet data laws to be passed". BBC. 2014.

[148] The Guardian, Theresa May unveils surveillance measures in wake of Snowden claims, 4 November 2015

European Union Charter of Fundamental Rights[149]. The European High Court took particular issue with sections 1 and 2 of the act which was going to allow the "security services through the Secretary of State to retain the powers to require a public telecommunications operator to retain communications data in line with the purposes of the Regulation of Investigatory Powers Act 2000."[150]

Due to the Data Retention and Investigatory Powers Act no longer being valid, the current regulation (the Investigatory Powers Act) grants powers almost similar to those in the Data Retention and Investigatory Powers Act. It grants the British intelligence services permission to carry out targeted interception of people's communications and requires internet service providers keep a log of accessed sites for British internet users for one year, amongst other things. However, with the new legislation, there are many checks and balances in play to ensure the powers given are not abused. These include measures such as the creation of an "Investigatory Powers Commission" to oversee the uses of the given powers and to ensure that the powers are not abused by the relevant intelligence agencies[151].

In the United Kingdom, there is also relevant case law governance in regards to the Internet Service Provider Obligations for National Security Reasons and specifically targeting the Investigatory Powers Tribunal. The main case to mention is the case of R (Privacy International) v <u>Investigatory Powers Tribunal</u>. In this case, the

[149]"Emergency surveillance law faces legal challenge from 2 MPs". BBC News

[150]Carly Nyst 2015 "Finally, the high court puts a brake on snooping on ordinary Britons". The Guardian

[151]"Investigatory powers bill: the key points". The Guardian. 4 November 2015.

government attempted to use legislation to prevent any judicial challenge or judicial appeal to any decision by the Investigatory Powers Tribunal[152]. The high court ruled that in an attempt to uphold the rule of law, no legislation shall be exempt from the checks and balances of the supreme court. This means that all spying complaints can be taken to supreme court and are not immune to being checked by the judiciary[153].

The United Kingdom's approach of having relevant checks and balances in place to prevent abuse of surveillance has advantages and disadvantages to it. One of the key strengths is that the United Kingdom's approach gives each individual heavy protection over their right to privacy. The presence of judicial oversight, allows for a non-biased system of checks and balances to ensure that the law is being upheld fairly and ensure the prevention of unfair targeting. Furthermore, the creation of the Investigatory Powers Commission helps hold relevant parties accountable for their actions and allows for great transparency. However, the United Kingdom's approach arguably does have a key disadvantage, this is that some might argue that due to all of the checks and balances in place, there is somewhat of a shield between malicious people and the intelligence services, terrorists may be able to abuse the systems protective methods and this may lead to avoidable deaths or injuries.

When making a comparison between the Chinese approach and the British approach, it's important to note both the similarities and differences of the approaches.

---

[152]R (on the application of Privacy International) v Investigatory Powers Tribunal and others [2019] UKSC 22

[153]Dawson, Joanna (28 May 2019). "What does the Supreme Court's ruling on the Investigatory Powers Tribunal mean for parliamentary sovereignty?". House of Commons Library.

The biggest similarity between the two approaches is that they both appear to seek to put obligations on internet service providers to ensure national security by means of covert surveillance on suspected residents. However, the Chinese approach is arguably more aggressive when compared to the British government's approach. The biggest difference between the two approaches is that the British approach is subjected to checks and balances through the different systems to ensure that the British intelligence services do not abuse the relevant surveillance laws whereas the Chinese legislations grants immense unchecked power over internet service providers to the security services. In conclusion, the legal approaches in China and the United Kingdom, in regards to internet service provider obligations for national security reasons, are very different due to the much broader powers with limited oversight granted to the Chinese security services in comparison to the much narrower powers and judicial oversight imposed on the British security services.

6 A COMPARISON OF JAPAN AND THE UNITED KINGDOM - WHAT ALLOWS FOR A VALID TERMINATION OF EMPLOYMENT?

<u>Introduction</u>

In this paper, I will discuss what validates a termination in the UK and Japan and make a comparison of the strictness or leniency of the terms of both countries' legislation and case law. Employment law in both respective countries is a key and important factor that is detrimental to the founding of a secure employment and thus, a secure livelihood. Stable employment provides a means of living for the employees as well as a means of running a business for an employer, so both the courts and legislation must be fair when it comes to what constitutes a valid termination. Regardless of the differences and similarities between the cultures of Japan and the UK, both countries must implement and uphold employment protections which are fair to both employers and employees.

<u>Japanese Employment Law - Establishing a Concrete Termination</u>

Japan's employment law, including the law regarding what constitutes a valid termination, has a few different pieces of the legislation which govern it. One of the most fundamental pieces of legislation was first introduced post-WW2, known as the Labor Standards Act. The Labor Standards act not only conveys many modern rights upon the workers of a company, but also sets some foundations on what constitutes a valid termination of employment. In regards to termination, one of the two key articles in this document is Article 19 which prevents an employer from dismissing an employee during a course of medical treatment for injury sustained during employment and an employer dismissing an employee for being absent for giving birth (pursuant to other articles)[154]. The second key article in the Labor standards act in regards to termination is article 20 which states that, subject to exceptions, "If an employer wishes to dismiss a worker, the employer must provide at least 30 days' advance notice. An employer not giving 30 days' advance notice must pay the worker the average wage they would earn in working for a period of at least 30 days"[155].

The second key piece of law which governs employment law, including the right of termination, is the Japanese Civil Code. Article 627 states some of the foundational terms of what would constitute a valid termination of employment and gives the examples of how much time of notice must be given from either party to commence termination[156]. Article 628, on the other hand, gives us our first insight into the actual grounds that would result in a termination of employment. It states that "Even if the parties have specified a term of employment, either party may immediately cancel the contract if there is a compelling reason to do so[157]". Given the lack of a definite answer as

---

[154]Labor Standards Act - Article 19
https://www.japaneselawtranslation.go.jp/en/laws/view/3567#je_ch2 at8

[155]Labor Standards Act - Article 20
https://www.japaneselawtranslation.go.jp/en/laws/view/3567#je_ch2 at8

[156]Civil Code - Article 627
https://www.japaneselawtranslation.go.jp/en/laws/view/3494/en#je_pt3ch2sc8at1

[157]Civil Code - Article 628

to what constitutes "a compelling reason", we must refer to case law to gather an answer.

One of the central terms when referring to employment termination in Japan is the concept of "just cause". This refers to the concept in Japanese employment law that, unless there is a just cause for termination, the termination will be ruled invalid. This is a stark contrast from jurisdictions such as America where "at will" termination is in place, allowing employers to terminate employment without a valid cause. The grounds of what constitutes a "just cause" is just as elusive as the definition for "a compelling reason", but the Toa Paint Case (1986) sheds some light on what could constitute a just cause. In this case, an employee who was responsible for sales was given an order to relocate but refused due to domestic circumstances. Because of his refusal, he was subjected to a disciplinary dismissal and this was deemed to be a valid dismissal by the courts[158]. This is one example of how a valid termination can be implemented. However, there usually is a difficulty in successfully terminating an employee due to the emphasis on Japan's cultural lifetime employment practice. This is emphasised by the Sega Enterprise Case (1999) in which an employee missed his business trip by oversleeping and then was transferred and failed to handle problems appropriately, which lead to a further transfer where multiple complaints were raised by clients featuring him and after a final transfer, he performed in bottom 10% of workers on 3 separate occasions and was terminated. However, the courts ruled his dismissal as invalid as the grounds to fire for "poor

---

https://www.japaneselawtranslation.go.jp/en/laws/view/3494/en#je_pt3ch2sc8at1

[158]Toa Paint Case (Decision by the Supreme Court, Second Petty Bench, July 14, 1986) https://www.mhlw.go.jp/file/06-Seisakujouhou-11200000-Roudoukijunkyoku/0000066935.pdf

performance" must mean really poor performance and in this case, there is still prospect of employee improvement[159]. Despite the difficulties in successfully terminating an employee for poor performance, there is a way that termination for employee performance is valid. The way to get around the stringent criteria for poor performance is the implementation of a probationary employment period. In the Japan Foundation Engineering Case (2012), an employee, who was still under the probationary period, had such poor performance that he endangered the life and limb of others as well as had poor awareness of timekeeping and compliance with rules. He had been given sufficient guidance and education from his employer to improve his ability but still failed and he was said to have no prospect of a dramatic improvement. His dismissal was ruled as valid by the courts[160]. One final case worth noting, when considering a valid termination of employment, is the Odakyu Densetsu Case (2003), in which an off-duty employee was arrested for touching a student inappropriately on a packed train. His dismissal was held to be valid but it was ruled that he must receive 30% of his severance allowance[161].

In conclusion, seeking a valid termination in Japan is difficult without the implementation of a probationary period or gross misconduct by the employee. Especially when performance is the main contributing factor, seeking

---

[159]Sega Enterprises Case (Decision by the Tokyo District Court, October 15, 1999) https://www.mhlw.go.jp/file/06-Seisakujouhou-11200000-Roudoukijunkyoku/0000066935.pdf

[160]Japan Foundation Engineering Case (Decision by Osaka High Court February 10, 2012) https://www.mhlw.go.jp/file/06-Seisakujouhou-11200000-Roudoukijunkyoku/0000066935.pdf

[161]Odakyu Electric Railway Incident (Tokyo High Court 1999) https://www.zenkiren.com/Portals/0/html/jinji/hannrei/shoshi/90010.html

a dismissal will not be an easy task for employers, given the cultural importance of the Japanese lifetime employment system.

UK Employment Law - Establishing a Concrete Termination

The UK's employment law is governed by case law and legislations, both of which are incredibly important. When referring to what constitutes a valid termination, one of the most important pieces of British legislation is the Employment Rights Act 1996. This piece of legislation importantly gives employees the right to have a reasonable notice before employment is terminated[162]. Furthermore, section 94 of the Employment Rights Act gives employees the right not to be unfairly dismissed. However, it is also stated that there is no restriction on management's right to dismiss, if the employee is just bad at his job or unpleasant to work with[163].

Historically, the only influence the courts had upon the concept of what constitutes a valid termination was through the case of Creen v Wright (1875), which ruled that employers have to give reasonable notice to employees prior to determination[164]. However, in recent times, the courts have begun to have a further and wider impact on the determination for a valid termination. The case of Wilson v Racher (1974) is a case which shows when a wrongful dismissal can take place. In this case, the employer consistently bullied the employee and when asking the employee to do a task, the employee snapped and swore at his employer. The court held that the

---

[162]Employment Rights Act 1996

[163]Employment Rights Act 1996

[164]Creen v Wright (1875) LR 1 CPD 591

employee's dismissal was invalid because the breakdown in trust and confidence was the employer's own doing[165]. Another instance in which the courts clarified the law regarding what constitutes a valid termination was in the case of Johnson v Unisys (2001), which helped to define when a termination is invalid during company reorganisation. In the aforementioned case, after 20 years of employment, Mr Johnson was dismissed for an alleged irregularity in his work. The courts ruled that the dismissal of employees during a company restructuring would be unfair if there is insufficient communication and consultation with affected staff[166]. One final case worth noting is the case of Kwik-Fit (GB) Ltd v Lineham (1992), wherein an employee used the work bathroom after hours and was scolded by his employer, so he threw his keys down, walked off and then later made a phone call saying that he would take the issue to tribunal. The employer saw this as a resignation and assumed that Lineham had quit the job and so claimed that the employee was unable to sue for unfair dismissal. The courts ruled that such an act does not constitute a voluntary dismissal[167].

In conclusion, the grounds for dismissal in the UK are very lenient. So long as sufficient notice is provided and an act of or general poor behaviour is existent, a termination can take place with not much chance that the courts will reverse the decision.

A Comparison of Japan and the UK

There are many similarities and differences that are displayed when comparing what constitutes a valid ground

---

[165]Wilson v Racher (1974) ICR 428

[166]Johnson v Unisys Limited (2001) UKHL 13

[167]Kwik-Fit (GB) Ltd v Lineham (1992) ICR 183

for terminating employment. Both systems aim to strike a balance between employee and employer protection. However, due to the numerous cultural factors and values to the society that influence each of the respective courts, the outcomes of certain cases would differ in the jurisdictions.

The first similarity between the countries is that both countries require a "just cause" to fire an employee and do not allow employees to be fired "at will". Both countries recognise that employee misconduct and very poor performance could constitute valid grounds for the termination of employment. However, even though this is the case, the scope of what defines terms such as "just cause" and "poor performance" vastly differs in the opposing nations. One example of this returns to the point of what constitutes a "just cause" to justify termination. It is strongly exposed by the differences between the Japanese Sega Enterprise Case (1999), in which an employee had multiple failings and complaints against him but was unable to have his contract terminated by the employer, and the UK guidance given under the British government, which states that you can even be dismissed if you have not been able to keep up with "changes to your job - for example, a new computer system" or even if you "cannot get along with your colleagues"[168].

The second similarity is that both countries also prohibit a termination from being held valid if the grounds for termination is that the employee was a whistleblower. In the UK, under the Employment Rights Act 1996, you cannot have a valid termination of employment on the grounds that an employee exposed "a criminal offence, a breach of legal duty, miscarriage of justice, health and safety violations, environmental damage, or deliberate

---

[168]https://www.gov.uk/dismissal/reasons-you-can-be-dismissed

concealment of wrongs"[169]. Similarly in Japan, the Whistleblower Protection Act 2004 is implemented to protect whistleblowers from unfair treatment and dismissal due to the actions that they take[170].

These points show that while the UK and Japan have differences in regards to their interpretations of specific terminology, both countries seek to uphold some similar practices such as the protection of whistleblowers or requiring notice to be given prior to employment termination.

Conclusion

In conclusion, the cultural differences between the opposing countries have led to significant differences on the view of different concepts such as poor performance. The concept of Japan's lifetime employment practice has lead to a much harsher view on what constitutes a valid ground for termination and seeks to uphold that, outside of redundancy, an employee can only be terminated if their presence in the company is a severe damage to the company by a display of employee misconduct or if their performance is so poor that it somehow goes far below that which was displayed in the Sega Enterprise case. In contrast, despite also wishing to protect both employees and employers alike, the UK takes the lenient approach that companies can terminate employment on grounds such as not being liked by coworkers or being suspected of committing wrongdoing. This highlights that while both the UK and the Japanese system have similar goals in mind, the approach and level of strictness to achieve this is completely different.

[169]Employment Rights Act 1996

[170]Whistleblower Protection Act (Act No. 122 of 2004) https://www.japaneselawtranslation.go.jp/en/laws/view/4220/en

7 THE LEGAL HISTORY OF BURAKUMIN DISCRIMINATION IN JAPAN

Introduction

In an unsuspecting town in Osaka, Japan, a mother awakens to hate mail posted through her door. It reads "We all hate you, no matter how many decades or centuries pass, we will continue to discriminate against you forever". During an interview, the woman stated "My children asked, 'Why is this happening to us? Why are we different?"[171] On the surface, Japan seems like an almost perfect society with little crime and a deep respect for the society as a whole and not just oneself. But there is an ongoing battle regarding discrimination in Japan today. A relic of Tokugawa Ieyasu's Edo's era, Burakumin discrimination. In this paper, I will be discussing the historical, societal and legal prejudices that have been faced by the class of people known as the Burakumin and the various attempts by both rights groups and the legal system at rectifying the mistakes of the past.

A Historical Background on the Burakumin

The discrimination of the Burakumin people arguably began at the beginning of the Edo period. At the beginning of the Edo period, Tokugawa Ieyasu introduced a social structure containing four classes based on Neo-

[171]https://www.independent.co.uk/news/world/asia/burakumin-descendants-of-caste-considered-tainted-face-new-discrimination-in-japan-a6791141.html

Confucianism, with Samurai holding the reigns as the top class[172]. However, another hidden 5th class formed outside of the structure, filled with the alleged "untouchables", known as the Burakumin. In the Shinto and Buddhist cultures in Japan, it was considered that working with any type of death polluted one's spirit and so occupations such as leatherworkers and executioners were seen as sub-human. Due to this, they were forced to live in hamlets, segregated from the general population.[173]

As the Edo period went on, the Burakumin people continued to suffer. The burakumin people were frequently used as scapegoats by the shogunate[174] and had legal restrictions imposed upon them such as mandated dress codes and hair styles so that they could be identified by the general population. By the beginning of the 18th century, the Burakumin peoples were prohibited from entering temples and schools, as well as the homes of members of the general population[175]. These changes were made to hold the Burakumin as the lowest class and keep them segregated from other Japanese citizens.

At the beginning of the Meiji restoration in the late 19th century, Japan began to abolish the feudal caste system. The government attempted to give some concessions to the Burakumin but the attempted integration of Burakumin into the general population was met was

---

[172]Neary, Ian (2003). ""Burakumin" at the End of History". Social Research.

[173]Meerman, Jacob (June 2, 2009). Socio-economic Mobility and Low-status Minorities: Slow Roads to Progress.

[174]Orbaugh, Sharalyn (2007). Japanese Fiction of the Allied Occupation: Vision, Embodiment, Identity

[175]Meerman, Jacob (June 2, 2009). Socio-economic Mobility and Low-status Minorities: Slow Roads to Progress

violence and backlash from commoners, who on many instances killed Burakumin who would enter their places of business[176].

The mindset against the Burakumin persisted and despite countless struggles, they would not be accepted by the general population.

Pre-Meiji Era Legal Discrimination

The pre-Meiji era saw the establishment of the Burakumin class as non-human in Japanese society. The Tokugawa shogunate implemented many laws that the Burakumin had to follow in order to widen the gap between the Burakumin and ordinary society. One such regulation was a regulation on marriage, according to the scholar Frank Upham, "Marriage outside the outcast group was at first simply not practised but later forbidden"[177]. Laws such as this were enacted to prevent the "pollution" of the Burakumin people from integrating with the general Japanese population. They were also forced to live in segregated communities and were not permitted to freely interact with the other classes[178].

Other regulations were also enacted upon the burakumin to keep them separate such as the previously mentioned legal restrictions imposed upon them such as mandated

---

[176]桐村 彰郎 (December 1, 1989). "Buraku kaihō hantai ikki ni miru minshū ishiki no shosō" 部落解放反対一揆にみる民衆意識の諸相 [Phases of Popular Consciousness in Riots against the Buraku Emancipation]. Nara Law Review

[177]Frank H. Upham, Law and Social Change in Post-War Japan (Cambridge, Massachusetts: Harvard University Press, 1987)

[178]Frank H. Upham, Law and Social Change in Post-War Japan (Cambridge, Massachusetts: Harvard University Press, 1987)

dress codes and hair styles so that they could be identified by the general population[179]. Furthermore, due to them being seen as non-human, the laws protecting them differed when compared to the other 4 classes and they could be "killed with impunity by members of the Samurai if they had committed a crime"[180]. Such discrimination continued up until the very end of the Pre-Meiji period with one magistrate in the mid-19th century stating that an Eta (Burakumin) is worth one seventh of an ordinary person[181].

Despite these terrors that ensued during the Edo period, the early attempts at legal reforms during the Meiji Era began to slowly unwind and set into motion the integration of the Burakumin into the general population.

The Meiji Reforms

In 1871, at the beginning of the Meiji era, the Meiji government issued the Senmin Haishirei ('Edict Abolishing Ignoble Classes') decree, giving outcasts equal legal status to the general population[182]. While this theoretically ended the caste system and should have led to full integration of the classes, the effect was not fully materialised.

---

[179]Meerman, Jacob (June 2, 2009). Socio-economic Mobility and Low-status Minorities: Slow Roads to Progress

[180]https://www.bbc.com/news/world-asia-34615972

[181]https://www.bbc.com/news/world-asia-34615972

[182]"Meijishonen ni okeru heigyūba shori-sei to to Chiku-Gyō - Hyōgo no jirei kara" 明治初年における斃牛馬処理制とと畜業 - 兵庫の事例から [The Slaughtering System and the Slaughtering Industry in the First Year of the Meiji Era: A Case of Hyogo]. Buraku Liberation and Human Rights Research Institute

At the beginning of the Meiji period, the consumption of meat was officially permitted and many of the Burakumin began to work as butchers. This led to many instances where butchers were discriminated against. There was even one instance where a group of men attempted to storm the emperor's palace after finding out that he had eaten meat[183].

Furthermore, despite the Burakumin now having equal status legally to the general population, societal biases and discrimination still remained. So much so, that the implementation of the edict abolishing the Burakumin class is cited as one of the secondary causes for the Blood Tax riots which lead to many Burakumin homes being burned down[184].

While theoretically ending the legal discrimination of Burakumin, the reforms of the Meiji era did not fully eliminate the Burakumin plight, as social attitudes continued to be against the Burakumin and the general population still looked upon Burakumin integration unfavourably.

Post-World War 2 Legal Reforms

The end of the second world war marked a complete restructuring of society under the allied occupation. The reforms that took place sought to further westernise Japan

---

[183]Harada, Nobuo (1993). Rekishi no naka no Amerika to niku shokumotsu to ten'nō sabetsu 歴史のなかの米と肉食物と天皇・差別 [Rice and Meat in History Food and the Emperor Discrimination]

[184]Howell, David L. (2005). Geographies of Identity in Nineteenth-Century Japan. Berkeley: University of California Press.

and promote the western values of democracy and equal rights for all. One of the key changes to Japanese society and the Japanese legal system was the introduction of the 1947 Constitution of Japan. The constitution states that "All people are equal under the law and there shall be no discrimination in political, economic or social relations because of race, creed, sex, social status or family origin."[185] By explicitly giving equal rights to all citizens, it adds another layer of legal protection to prevent discrimination against Burakumin.

While the new constitution sought to enshrine western values into Japan, the discrimination against Burakumin continued. As Japan modernised and developed, Burakumin were left behind and standards of life for the Burakumin lagged behind the general Japanese population but this was noticed and the government attempted to rectify the situation with the 1969 Special Measures Law for Assimilation Projects[186] which provided funding for the Burakumin communities.

However, even in modern times, the government is still introducing measures to prevent discrimination against Burakumin. Prior to 2008, it was relatively easy to get a copy of another person's family koseki. This made it easy for interested parties to discover who the descendants of Burakumin were and continue to discriminate against them generationally. However, in May 2008, the Law on Family Registry was implemented, which limited the people who can access another person's koseki[187].

---

[185]Constitution of Japan 1947

[186]"Hōritsu dai roku jū-gō (Akira shi shi nana ichi rei) dōwa taisaku jigyō tokubetsu sochi-hō" 法律第六十号(昭四四・七・一〇) 同和対策事業特別措置法 [Law No. 60 (Showa 44.7.10) Dowa countermeasures business special measures law]. 1969 The House of Representatives, Japan

The most recent legal attempt to put an end to the discrimination of the Burakumin was the enactment of the Act on the Promotion of the Elimination of Buraku Discrimination[188] in 2016, with the purpose of promoting "the elimination of Buraku discrimination and thereby realising a society free from Buraku discrimination."

The Buraku Liberation League

After the second world war, the National Committee for Burakumin Liberation had begun and in the 1950's, changed its name to the Buraku Liberation League. The introduction of the Buraku Liberation League arguably played an important role in securing change for the Burakumin.

They would consistently lobby the government for concessions and its recognition of Burakumin discrimination in Japan. In 1961 they got their first major achievement with the Japanese government enacting the 'Law to Establish a Deliberative Council for Buraku Assimilation' which was incredibly crucial as it was the first time ever that the government publicly admitted that Buraku discrimination existed[189].

However, despite continuing to lobby for a good cause, valid criticisms arose in the early days regarding the group.

---

[187] Law on Family Registry, Article 10

[188] Act on the Promotion of the Elimination of Buraku Discrimination (Act No. 109 of 2016)

[189] 1965 Report of the Integration Measures Deliberation Council, English translation, as cited in Karin Buhmann, Civil and Political Rights in Japan (Denmark: The Danish Center of Human Rights, 1989)

For example, some early members of the group would commit acts of violence and kidnapping[190]. One key incident was the Yatsuka incident of 1974, where teachers and students of a high school were attacked at random if they were not outspoken about support for the Burakumin Liberation League[191]. Though these kinds of displays are arguably counterproductive to the cause, in modern times the Burakumin Liberation League has shifted away from methods like this and as of 1988, is designated as a human rights NGO by the United Nations.

Changing Societal Attitudes

In modern Japan, many Japanese people believe wholeheartedly that Burakumin discrimination is no longer existent. This belief is backed up by many actions such as the disbanding of the Zenkairen (another Burakumin liberation group) in 2004 when they announced that "the Buraku issue has basically been resolved"[192]. Furthermore, one of the important topics regarding Burakumin rights was marriage discrimination but in modern times, an estimated between 60 to 80% of burakumin marry a non-burakumin, which is a massive increase since the early 1940s, where the rate was estimated at 10%[193]. But it's important to note that while discrimination against

---

[190]Upham, Frank K. (2009). Law and Social Change in Postwar Japan. Harvard University Press.

[191]The Association for the Protection of the Truth of Yatsuka "The Truth of the Yatsuka High School Incident: Report from Tajima" (Buraku Affairs Research Institute Publishing Department, 1978.3)

[192]"Zenkoku Buraku Kaihou Undou Rengkai" (National Buraku Liberation Alliance) (2004), "Zenkairen Dai 34 Kai Teiki Taikai Ni Tuite" ('About the Zenkairen 34th Regular Meeting)

[193]https://www.nancho.net/kyoto/nadamoto.html

Burakumin has arguably lessened to a large degree, it has not been eradicated and incidents of Burakumin discrimination often take place in the Japanese political world. One well known event occurred in 2001 when two candidates to succeed the premier of Japan had to be decided. Hiromu Nonaka was one of the two candidates. During a meeting of LDP officials, the opposing candidate reportedly told the party "We are not going to let someone from the Buraku become the prime minister, are we?"[194]

It is also important to note that while discrimination against Burakumin in the modern day is not as prevalent as it once was, a government survey conducted back in 1965 found that 70% of people thought that burakumin were of a different race than other Japanese people.[195] While such an idea may seem outlandish to us now, it's important to remember that this still took place in recent history.

The last area of discrimination against the Burakumin which is of primary concern is employment discrimination. One infamous example of this in recent history occurred in 1975, when a book titled 'A Comprehensive List of Buraku Area Names' was exposed as being sold to companies, in order for employers to identify and avoid hiring Burakumin[196]. However, the incident was quickly publicised and a denunciation meeting was held with representatives of the purchasing companies who were chastised for their behaviour[197].

---

[194]Yamaguchi, Mari, "Discrimination claims die hard in Japan", The Japan Times, January 25, 2009

[195]"Peasants, Rebels, Women and Outcastes: the Underside of Modern Japan," Mikiso Hane, Rowman and Littlefield 2003

[196]終わってはいない「部落地名総鑑」事件
部落解放同盟中央本部 1995年12月 (The unfinished "Buraku Gazetteer" case, Buraku Liberation League Central Headquarters, December 1995)

However, in more recent times, employment opportunities continue to not be as existent as they are for regular Japanese citizens. Burakumin usually work irregular jobs and are forced to do undesired jobs due to financial needs. After the Fukushima disaster of 2011, it has been claimed that many of the Burakumin were hired to clean the nuclear waste as many are in poverty and had no choice but to take the job if they needed money[198]. The use of unskilled temporary employees (in a lot of cases, Burakumin) who are sent to nuclear power plants to deal with high levels of radiation was commented on by a city councilman who said "It's wrong to prey on the poor who need to feed their families. They're considered disposable, and that's immoral."[199]

Recommendations

Whilst differing opinions occur on the issue, it's my belief that a multi-layered approach is needed to combat the remnants of Burakumin discrimination.

My first recommendation is to continue to strengthen legislation against Burakumin discrimination. This requires a two-stage approach to handle two widely different issues. The first stage targets criminal legislation. I believe that by strengthening punishments for Burakumin discrimination is a good way to deter discriminatory messages being sent

---

[197]Representatives of 103 companies on the stage denounced discriminatory book purchases "Asahi Shimbun" March 1977, 52

[198]Minority Rights Group International, State of the World's Minorities and Indigenous Peoples 2013 - Case study: Japan's Burakumin minority hired to clean up after Fukushima, 24 September 2013

[199]https://www.latimes.com/archives/la-xpm-2011-dec-04-la-fg-japan-nuclear-gypsies-20111204-story.html

to Burakumin. The second stage tackles the crucial issue of employment discrimination. I believe that as long as books such as 'A Comprehensive List of Buraku Area Names' exist, employment discrimination against Burakumin will be hard to root out. While this could arguably be solved by the passage of time, as many Burakumin marry non-burakumin and change their family names, as well as members of historically Burakumin communities moving home and migrating to other communities, I believe that for the complete eradication of Burakumin employment discrimination, there needs to be an overhaul of the employment application system in Japan and there needs to be a mandatory way to protect people's personal details during the first stages of employment application procedure.

The second layer of the approach is to target the problem of how historical Burakumin are viewed. Without the Burakumin, many great armies would have had no leather and Japanese history could have been completely different. It's important to recognise the contributions to society that both historical and Burakumin had and how the modern descendants of Burakumin also contribute heavily to society.

Conclusion

In conclusion, Burakumin discrimination is a potent type of discrimination that dates back to the historical Edo period and has remained unextinguished since. The historical legal rights of Burakumin were little, as they were not even recognised as having the full value of a human until the Meiji period. However, even such legal changes did not assist in influencing the view of Japanese society on those who were formerly known as the 5th class. The post-war activism and concessions given by the governments helped to heavily drive down Burakumin discrimination and provide Burakumin with opportunities equal to that of any other Japanese citizen. However, despite the decline in discriminatory views, discrimination still takes place in some instances that happen in the open, such as hate mail being sent to residents of historically Burakumin areas, and behind closed doors, such as what occurred during the Nonoka incident in Japanese politics. However, I believe that the continual and rapid shift in recent Japanese views, in its current trajectory, will lead to a near-end of Burakumin discrimination in the near future.

8 THE OKINAWAN RIGHT TO SELF-DETERMINATION – PROBLEMS PRESENTED BY THE UNITED STATES MILITARY PRESENCE AND A FLURRY OF AMERICAN HUMAN RIGHTS ABUSES

Introduction

In this paper, I will explore the human rights issue of the right to self-determination of the Okinawan people. It is important to note that I will not be discussing whether the right of Okinawa to secede from Japan exists, but instead I will discuss the Okinawan right to self-determination in regards to the presence of American Military bases and personnel from the island and the issues presented by America's presence. Okinawa itself harbours a unique historical and political situation as well as bearing a heavy burden that does not affect any mainland Japanese location in the same way due to its post-WW2 status. I hope that this paper can shed light on the implications of a permanent foreign military presence in Okinawa and why Okinawa should have the right to self-determine whether a foreign military presence is stationed on the island.

Historical Context

Before I begin to discuss the modern impact of Okinawa's lack of self-determination, it is important to delve into the history of Okinawa, in order to gain a greater understanding of how the current situation came to be.

During the second world war, Okinawa was the only part of Japan that was invaded and occupied prior to the Japanese surrender. During the American invasion, one third of Okinawa's civilian population were killed[200]. This led to the beginning of Okinawa's unique situation. After the war had ended, the US set up a military administration to rule Okinawa under a trusteeship and during this period set up numerous military bases. During the 1950s, the American Military used their power to forcefully seize land from Okinawans in order to build new military bases, displacing over 250,000 Okinawans in order to assert dominance at the beginning of the cold war[201]. Attitudes against the American Military presence in Okinawa began to exacerbate after the 1955 rape and murder of a 6 year old girl by an American soldier which was then followed by another rape of a child by another American soldier one week later which lead to mass protests against American military presence[202]. During the cold war, the Americans also then began to store nuclear weapons in Okinawa, despite the Japanese public being firmly against it[203].

---

[200]The Economist (November 3 2005). No home where the dugong roam. The Economist.
https://www.economist.com/asia/2005/10/27/no-home-where-the-dugong-roam

[201]Special Subcommittee of the Armed Services Committee, House of Representatives (1955). "The Melvin Price Report"

[202]Kawato, Yuko (April 8 2015). Protests Against U.S. Military Base Policy in Asia: Persuasion and Its Limits. Stanford, Calif.: Stanford University Press, 2015. xvi, 224 pp. ISBN: 9780804794169. The Journal of Asian Studies, 75(4), 1107–1108.
https://doi.org/10.1017/s0021911816001248

[203]Mitchell, Jon (January 2013). "Herbicide Stockpile" at Kadena Air Base, Okinawa: 1971 U.S. Army report on Agent Orange. The Asia-Pacific Journal: Japan Focus. https://apjjf.org/2013/11/1/Jon-Mitchell/3883/article.html

Legal Essays

The beginning of the Vietnam war during the postwar era significantly influenced the controversy of the placement of nuclear weapons in Okinawa. During the Vietnam war, due to the vicinity of Okinawa to Vietnam, Okinawa was used as a key staging point by the American army in regards to military operations that would take place. The strategic importance of Okinawa's location and its close vicinity to mainland Asia, led the US to remain as a military presence in Okinawa[204]. During this time, Okinawa and its residents began to view the US as a much more aggressive and warmongering force as opposed to playing a peacekeeper role[205].

Prior to the islands being returned to Japan in 1972, there were several other incidents during the Vietnam war that influenced Okinawan attitudes towards American Military bases. However, none of which portray the presence of the American Military bases in a good light.

The Impact on Okinawan Society

In this section I will discuss some of the impact on Okinawan society that has been presented by the presence of American Military bases. In particular, the social and cultural disruptions as well as environmental concerns posed by the residents. The overwhelming presence of the American Military bases has been proven to <u>disproportionately affect the peo</u>ple and environment of

[204]John Morrocco. Rain of Fire. (United States: Boston Publishing Company)

[205]Trumbull, R. (August 1 1965). OKINAWA B-52'S ANGER JAPANESE; Bombing of Vietnam from island stirs public outcry. The New York Times.
https://www.nytimes.com/1965/08/01/archives/okinawa-b52s-anger-japanese-bombing-of-vietnam-from-island-stirs.htmls

Okinawa. Even though Okinawa only comprises roughly 0.6% of Japan's land mass, 75% of American Military bases in Japan are placed in Okinawa[206].

One of the environmental impacts that are caused by the presence of American Military bases is the damage to land and sea caused by negligence. There are occasionally oil leaks which damage the Okinawan wildlife and has led to water contamination, and hazardous materials are now often detected in the soil of farmland where American Military technology has fallen[207]. One recent example of negligence by the American Military occurred in 2020 when it was discovered that they are leaking PFA's (a cancer-causing substance) from Kaneda Air Force Base into the water supply, which has affected 450,000 people's water, a third of Okinawa's residents[208]. However, instead of recognising and apologising for creating such a problem, the American Military stated that it would be inappropriate to speculate on the origin of the leaks, despite the only capable source of contamination being the air force base and all evidence pointing towards it. The American Military then refused to allow Okinawan government officials to investigate the cause of the pollution, despite previous reports showing that between 2001 and 2005, 23,000 litres of various foams were mistakenly released by the American Military[209].

---

[206]Rabson, Steve (February 2008), "Okinawan Perspectives on Japan's Imperial Institution", The Asia-Pacific Journal

[207]https://www.pref.okinawa.jp/site/kankyo/seisaku/kikaku/documents/2-4.pdf

[208]Mitchell, Jon (August 2020). PFAS Contamination from US Military Facilities in Mainland Japan and Okinawa. The Asia-Pacific Journal: Japan Focus. https://apjjf.org/2020/16/JMitchell.html

[209]Mitchell, J. (October 12 2020). US military bases are poisoning Okinawa. The Diplomat. https://thediplomat.com/2020/10/us-military-bases-are-poisoning-

Furthermore, there is no environmental compliance required of the American Military in Japan as they are not subject to Japanese law and so are able to commit violations and behave carelessly. Even when the American Military returns land to civilian use, treaties between Japan and America exempts it from the need to conduct clean-ups. Between 2003 and 2018, Japanese tax-payers paid out 13 billion yen to clean up former bases on Okinawa, many of which were tainted with toxins such as dioxin, asbestos and lead[210]. Another problem caused to the environment is caused by the leakage of the horrific chemical compound 'Agent Orange', reports have indicated that more than a third of the barrels stored in Okinawa have developed leaks and this has led Okinawans to ask for environmental investigations, but as of 2012 both Japan and America refused to investigate[211].

One of the social disruptions is caused by the testing of military equipment in populated areas. Particularly, the frequent fighter jets. A study conducted in 2010 investigated the effects of the prolonged exposure to aircraft noise around the Kadena Air Base instalment and found that they have led to causes of health issues to the Okinawan people, such as a disrupted sleep pattern, high blood pressure, weakening of the immune system in children, and a loss of hearing[212]. Furthermore, the

---

okinawa/https://thediplomat.com/2020/10/us-military-bases-are-poisoning-okinawa/

[210]The Mainichi (December 17 2018). Japan gov't has paid nearly 13 bil. yen since FY 2003 on Okinawa US base land cleanup. The Mainichi. https://mainichi.jp/english/articles/20181217/p2a/00m/0na/025000c

[211]Mitchell, Jon (September 2012). Agent Orange on Okinawa - The Smoking Gun: U.S. army report, photographs show 25,000 barrels on island in early '70s. The Asia-Pacific Journal: Japan Focus. https://apjjf.org/2012/10/40/Jon-Mitchell/3838/article.html

[212]Cox, R. (2010). The Sound of Freedom: US military aircraft noise in

American Military bases are often situated in the centre of densely populated areas. For example, Kadena Air Base constitutes around 83% of the land area of Kadena Town, which forces more than 10,000 residents to squeeze into the remaining 17 percent of the land. The town houses, schools, hospitals and other facilities are tightly squeezed into the small areas within only several hundred metres of the runways of the base[213]. Another issue harming the social society of Okinawa is the damage to the economy caused by American Military presence. Okinawa is the Japanese prefecture with the highest level of poverty and the American Military bases hold some of the blame for this[214]. Statistics showed that the bases accounted for up to 5% of the Okinawan economy. However, because the US bases take up 20% of Okinawa's land, they impose a deadweight loss of 15% on the Okinawan economy, hampering the already poverty-stricken prefecture[215]. On top of this, mainland Japan has cut funding for Okinawa when the residents elect anti-military politicians. This happened in 2015, when the national government announced that Okinawa's funding will be cut, due to the residents of Okinawa electing a governor who had the desire to remove the American Military bases from Okinawa[216]. Such a horrendous act would likely be

---

Okinawa, Japan. Anthropology News, 51(9), 13–14. https://doi.org/10.1111/j.1556-3502.2010.51913.x

[213]Japanese Communist Party,. (February 2000). Problems of U.S. military bases in Okinawa.
https://www.jcp.or.jp/seisaku/gaiko_anpo/Okinawa.pdf

[214]Siripala, T. (May 24 2022). 50 years after US occupation, Okinawa continues to resist military bases. The Diplomat.
https://thediplomat.com/2022/05/50-years-after-us-occupation-okinawa-continues-to-resist-military-bases/

[215]Taira, Koji (1997). "The Okinawan charade: The United States, Japan and Okinawa: Conflict and Compromise, 1995-1996," Japan Policy Research Institute, Working Paper, No 28.

chastised worldwide if Russia or China decided to cut funding to their poorest region because its residents elected a politician who would like to refuse to allow a warmongering force to displace their citizens and use their land as a springboard for war. It's a horrific attempt of blackmailing and twisting the democratic right to vote that the people of Okinawa possess.

However, the main issue, which I will discuss in detail in this next segment is the general behaviour of American personnel who are given special privileges when in Okinawa and are known to frequently commit crimes and behave poorly and in some cases even later boast about the crimes[217] which has had an effect on the social life of Okinawans.

Highlighted Human Rights Abuses Conducted by American Soldiers

Many individual human rights abuses are caused by American military personnel stationed in Okinawa, who often use the strength of their nation to avoid being punished. The human rights abuses date all the way back to the end of the second world war, where large numbers of American soldiers were accused of rape[218]. One

---

[216] Reynolds, I., & Takahashi, M. (January 14 2015). Japan cuts Okinawa budget after election of Anti-Base governor. Bloomberg.com. https://www.bloomberg.com/news/articles/2015-01-14/japan-cuts-okinawa-budget-after-election-of-anti-base-governor

[217] https://imadr.org/wordpress/wp-content/uploads/2013/01/No.-10-world.pdf

[218] Tanaka, Yuki (2003). Japan's Comfort Women: Sexual Slavery and Prostitution during World War II and the U.S. Occupation. (Asia's Transformations.) New York: Routledge. 2002. Pp. xix, 212. The American Historical Review. https://doi.org/10.1086/ahr/108.4.1122

highlighted incident included three African-American soldiers who would frequently rape women of the Katsuyama village[219] and terrorise the villages, which led the residents to be forced to recruit the aid of two soldiers of the Imperial Japanese Army, who were hiding in the jungle, to enact justice[220]. Such instances were repeated constantly during the American occupation of Okinawa. One highly publicised incident in Okinawa was the 1955 Yumiko incident, where the rape and murder of a 5 year old girl by an American soldier stationed in Okinawa made headlines. The perpetrator stood trial only 14 days after a different American marine was sentenced for raping a 9 year old Okinawan girl[221]. In the Yumiko incident, the Americans stated that they would give him the death penalty. However, he was later extradited to America, the promised death penalty was cancelled and he was released some years later. To add salt upon the wounds, after passing away, the perpetrator was given an honourable headstone provided by the US department of veteran affairs, marking him for his service in World War 2, despite being a convicted rapist and murderer. This was met with fury from Okinawan activists when it was uncovered in 2021[222].

---

[219]Sims, Calvin (June 1 2000). 3 Dead Marines and a Secret of Wartime Okinawa. The New York Times.
https://www.nytimes.com/2000/06/01/world/3-dead-marines-and-a-secret-of-wartime-okinawa.html

[220]Cullen, L. (August 13 2001). "Okinawa Nights". Time.
https://content.time.com/time/subscriber/article/0,33009,170085,00.html

[221]Pasadena Independent. (November 23 1955) "Hurt". Pasadena Independent. https://www.newspapers.com/article/pasadena-independent-hurt/99298081/

[222]Okinawa Times (2021) "刑期の半分以下「異常だ」仮釈放されていた幼女殺害の米兵「沖縄で起きたことだからか」怒りの声 |

Such behaviour occurs in modern times, even after Okinawa's return to Japan. The most famous incident occurred in 1995, where three African-American soldiers decided to abduct, beat up and gang rape a 12 year old Okinawan girl for sexual gratification[223]. There was then criticism from the families of the rapists, who tried to claim that the rapists are being targeted for being black[224], but these remarks were later retracted. One of the key points of outrage of this case, was that it brought recognition to the US-Japan Status of Forces Agreement, which exempts American soldiers from the jurisdiction of Japanese law[225]. Japanese police immediately requested to transfer custody of the rapists to Japanese authorities, but the American army initially refused and then delayed this as much as possible and did not transfer the rapists to be charged for over 20 days[226]. This delay caused large

---

沖縄タイムス＋プラス プレミアム". 沖縄タイムス＋プラス
https://www.okinawatimes.co.jp/articles/-/835340

[223]Watanabe, T. (March 5 2019). Okinawa Rape Suspect's Lawyer Gives Dark Account□: Japan: Attorney of accused Marine says co-defendant admitted assaulting 12-year-old girl "just for fun." Los Angeles Times. https://www.latimes.com/archives/la-xpm-1995-10-28-mn-62075-story.html

[224]Watanabe, T. (March 5 2019). Wife Pleads Marine's Case in Okinawa Rape Trial□: Justice: Spouse says her husband, accused in brutal attack on schoolgirl, is a gentle and intelligent man. Los Angeles Times. https://www.latimes.com/archives/la-xpm-1995-12-05-mn-10474-story.html

[225]Administrative Agreement under Article III of the Security Treaty between Japan and the United States of America. https://worldjpn.net/documents/texts/docs/19520228.T1E.html

[226]The Associated Press. (September 29 1995). Americans charged in rape in Okinawa. The New York Times. https://www.nytimes.com/1995/09/29/world/americans-charged-in-rape-in-okinawa.html

protests in Okinawa, which lead to the American military agreeing that in future, they can consider transferring suspects immediately, if the severity of the crime justifies it[227].

These are not just isolated incidents, American military personnel consistently behave poorly and commit crimes, protected by the American war machine's strongarm over mainland Japan and Okinawa. Between 1972 and 2009, American army personnel committed over 5,600 criminal offenses, including 25 murders, 385 burglaries, 25 arsons, 127 rapes, 306 assaults[228]. However, critics have argued that due to rapes being vastly under-reported, the actual amount is much higher[229]. The problem posed such a threat to Okinawan life that in 2013, Toru Hashimoto, the former mayor of Osaka, advocated for an increase in the Okinawan adult entertainment sector, stating that "Unless they make use of these facilities, it will be difficult to control the sexual energies of the wild Marines"[230]. A spokesperson from a women civil rights group in Okinawa stated "A sex crime occurs, politicians are outraged, the US military apologises. Then it happens again. And it's going

---

[227]Watanabe, T. (March 5 2019). U.S., Japan OK pact on military crime suspects. Los Angeles Times. https://www.latimes.com/archives/la-xpm-1995-10-26-mn-61240-story.html

[228]Hearst, D. (November 26 2017). Second battle of Okinawa looms as China's naval ambition grows. The Guardian.
https://www.theguardian.com/world/2011/mar/07/okinawa-japan-military-tension

[229]Women for Genuine Security. "Okinawa: Effects of long-term US Military presence" (PDF).
http://www.genuinesecurity.org/partners/report/Okinawa.pdf

[230]Slavin, E. (14 May 2013). "Osaka mayor: 'Wild Marines' should consider using prostitutes". Stars and Stripes.
http://www.stripes.com/news/pacific/bad-behavior-in-the-pacific/osaka-mayor-wild-marines-should-consider-using-prostitutes-1.220845

to continue to happen until the wording of the Status of Forces Agreement changes"[231].

Whilst most-probably the majority of American soldiers behave in an acceptable manner, enough of them behave recklessly, knowing they are protected by the American government and the Status of Forces Agreement, for it to be considered damaging to the safety of Okinawan people, particularly women and children.

Legal Framework

It is important to also discuss the legal frameworks applicable to the Okinawan right to self-determination. There are various treaties, international laws and national laws that could affect the Okinawan right to self-determine whether a foreign countries military bases remain.

We must first recognise that the right to self-determination is one of the universal rights of international law. Even the founding charter of the UN states that the purpose of its existence is "to develop friendly relations among nations based on respect for the principle of equal rights and self-determination of peoples"[232]. Okinawa, being part of Japan, is also given these principles and rights which should allow Okinawan individuals universally granted rights and freedoms.

Under international law, the people of Okinawa should

---

[231]Hernon, M. (April 22 2022). US marine indicted for sexual assault in Okinawa. Tokyo Weekender.
https://www.tokyoweekender.com/japan-life/news-and-opinion/us-marine-indicted-for-sexual-assault-in-okinawa/

[232]United Nations, Charter of the United Nations (1945)
https://www.refworld.org/docid/3ae6b3930.html1945.

have the right to determine their own sovereignty and international political status with no interference[233]. However, despite being bound by these rules, this has not been respected by mainland Japan. One prominent example of this was displayed in 1994 when the Okinawan peoples elected a governor who opposed the construction of new American military bases. However, the mainland Japanese government was not happy with this and grossly and openly violated international law by successfully suing the governor of Okinawa and transferring control over Okinawan land leases to the prime minister of Japan, ignoring the 1997 referendum rejecting new military bases and ceasing communication and economic support to Okinawa until the people elected a member of the LDP (the party ruling the mainland Japanese government) as the governor[234].

National law is also arguably in stark contrast with the presence of the American military in Okinawa. The foundation of the Japanese legal system is the Japanese constitution, which has not undergone any major changes since its conception. Article 9 of the Japanese constitution states "Aspiring sincerely to an international peace based on justice and order, the Japanese people forever renounce war as a sovereign right of the nation and the threat or use of force as means of settling international disputes"[235]. The Japanese courts have defined this as meaning that Japan can have no offensive weapons such as nuclear weapons

---

[233]United Nations, Charter of the United Nations (1945) https://www.refworld.org/docid/3ae6b3930.html1945.

[234]Dietz, Kelly. (2016). Transnationalism and Transition in the Ryūkyūs. In: Iacobelli, P., Leary, D., Takahashi, S. Transnational Japan as History. Palgrave Macmillan Transnational History Series. Palgrave Macmillan, New York.
https://doi.org/10.1007/978-1-137-56879-3_10

[235]Constitution of Japan - Article 9

(such as those placed in Okinawa by the American military)[236]. By using Okinawa as a springboard of war and offensive weapons, the spirit of Article 9 is being violated and the Japanese commitment to pacifism is seen as nothing but empty words. This should prompt an examination of the constitutionality of the American military presence in Okinawa.

Okinawan Attitudes to the American Military Presence

Due to the troubled World War 2 history with America and the consistent crimes conducted by members of the American military, the general population of Okinawa are strongly against the American military presence. According to a 2007 poll conducted by the Okinawan Times, 85% of Okinawans oppose the presence of the American military on Okinawa[237]. These attitudes are shown time and time again in every poll conducted on the matter. In another poll conducted by The Asahi Shimbun in May 2010, 43% of the Okinawan population wanted the complete closure of the American military bases, 42% of the population wanted reduction, and only 11% wanted to maintain status quo[238].

The Okinawan people also constantly display their

---

[236]Writer, S. (June 3 2022). Japan to develop combat drones to assist jet fighters. Nikkei Asia. https://asia.nikkei.com/Politics/Japan-to-develop-combat-drones-to-assist-jet-fighters

[237]Okinawa Times (May 13 2007). 語り継ぎたい「沖縄戦」 https://web.archive.org/web/20070930160334/http://www.okinawatimes.co.jp/edi/20070513.html

[238]Asahi.com (May 23 2010)
"普天間移設首相方針、県民７６％反対 朝日新聞世論調査". https://web.archive.org/web/20100523062343/http://www.asahi.com/politics/update/0513/SEB201005130037.html

opinions through political elections where the candidates against the positioning of American bases in Okinawa practically always win. As early as 2018, Denny Tamaki was elected as the next governor of Okinawa prefecture, after a campaign focused mainly on the vast reduction the American military presence on the island[239]. There have been many referendums on the matter but they are almost always ignored by the mainland Japanese government. In 2019, in an Okinawan referendum voting on the construction of another American military base in Okinawa, over 70% of people voted against the construction. However, following the results, the prime minister of Japan said he planned to press forward and called for an understanding from Okinawan citizens.

It is also important to note that it is not just Okinawa that does not want American military bases present on its land, this sentiment is seemingly shared by all Japanese prefectures. Even back in 1955, Tokyo citizens successfully prevented an American military base expansion in Tachikawa through mass protests in an incident known as the Sunagawa Struggle[240]. This goes to show that the nation of Japan does not want to bear the burden of the presence of American military forces.

Potential Solutions

---

[239]Denyer, S. (September 30 2018). Opponent of U.S. military bases wins Okinawa gubernatorial election. Washington Post.
https://www.washingtonpost.com/world/asia_pacific/opponent-of-us-military-bases-wins-okinawa-gubernatorial-election/2018/09/30/18f13d5a-c36a-11e8-9451-e878f96be19b_story.html

[240]Wright, D. (June 1 2015). "Sunagawa Struggle" ignited anti-U.S. base resistance across Japan. The Japan Times.
https://www.japantimes.co.jp/community/2015/05/03/issues/sunagawa-struggle-ignited-anti-u-s-base-resistance-across-japan/

There are a variety of ways to resolve the problem for Okinawa. I would like to propose three potential solutions to fixing the problem. They are; The Humanitarian Approach, The Nationalist Approach and The Pacifist Approach.

The Humanitarian Approach focuses on the safeguarding and protection of the Okinawan people, while at the same time keeping Japan well-protected from foreign invasion and continuing to respect the status quo with some justified changes. For this approach, I propose keeping the American military presence in Okinawa but removing all of the protections and concessions given to soldiers of the American military so that they will be subject to the law to the exact same extent as a Japanese citizen allowing the Okinawan peoples to feel safer, while also protecting mainland Japan from bearing the burden of hosting the American military to such a heavy amount. Furthermore, I would propose a mandatory heavy tax on the American military for using the islands of Okinawa. This would allow the American military to fix the drain that they economically cause on Okinawa and make right the poverty that they are causing.

The Nationalist Approach focuses on the removal of the American military from Japan and the redemption of Japanese military sovereignty. This would involve revoking Article 9 of the Japanese Constitution and giving the American military a set time period to withdraw all troops from Japan. During this time, Japan should bolster its military capacity and take over the positions which the American military leaves. While this likely is not the most popular opinion, it allows Japan to regulate the conduct of its own soldiers and punish misbehaving soldiers appropriately. Furthermore, it allows Japan to be aware of the environmental issues caused by military presence in

Okinawa and act accordingly and most probably more sensibly than the American military.

The Pacifist Approach focuses on the removal of the American military from Japan and the upholding of the Japanese Constitution. This would involve upholding Article 9 of the Japanese Constitution but also asserting to the American military that they have a set time period to withdraw all forces from Japan. This would protect the safety of the Okinawan people and environment while maintaining the Japanese status-quo position as a nation against war. However, this approach would leave Japan vulnerable to unlikely but existent external nuclear threats and therefore is my least recommended proposition.

I believe that any three of my proposed solutions would likely have a positive effect on the Okinawan region and the Japanese nation as a whole but it would be impossible to tell without their actual implementation.

Conclusion

In conclusion, there are many problems presented by the American military presence in Okinawa, in regards to both environmental problems caused by negligence, and criminal problems caused by poor conduct from American soldiers. Furthermore, it is evident that the overwhelming majority of Okinawans do not want the American military to be there. They are forced to bear a heavy burden that no other part of Japan wants to bear. Their constant votes against the American military have gone unheard and ignored by the mainland Japanese government. Therefore, it is painfully clear that the minimum requirement for Americans to be stationed in Okinawa should be that they are provided with less protections and concessions. Okinawa has the right to the universal human right of self-determination and this right has not been provided. If we look at previous historical trends like the rationale for the UK leaving the EU, taking away a people's right to determine their own laws only leads to frustration and the cessation of those peoples away from the greater union. If Japan values Okinawa remaining as a part of Japan, it is highly advisable that they look at my suggestions for guidance to resolve the problem.

9 COMPARING LEGAL INHERITANCE PRINCIPLES IN JAPAN AND ENGLAND: PRIORITY LAWS, PROPERTY WITH NO VALID INHERITOR AND THE INSTANCE OF AN INHERITORS DEATH

Introduction

In this paper, I will be making a comparative study of Japan and the United Kingdom. I will be focusing on the procedure of inheritance. However, I will have a focus on exploring some areas with little-to-no current academic research in regards to comparing the two nations. The first of which I wish to focus on, is what happens to an estate when there is no valid inheritor to be found. If somebody passes away and they have no successors or close relatives, will the land be given to the state by default or is there a different method of determining what happens with the land? The second key point I wish to focus on, is the English law principle of Jus Accrescendi, which is the ruling procedure of determining what happens to a shared stake in a property upon an inheritor's death where multiple inheritors are present.

Priority Laws (First Instance)

The first key area that I must speak about is priority law. These are the laws which govern the immediate procedure of inheritance. In this section, I will discuss the first instances of inheritance prior to the distribution of property to family inheritors. This includes things such as debts and claims, so that any person or entity who is owed money, can get their funding returned prior to the distribution of the estate to the family and friends. This section will compare the procedures between Japan and the United Kingdom, in regards to the first instance of priority laws.

In the case of an English national passing away in the United Kingdom, the right of priority is governed by the United Kingdom's Government Guidelines. According to the guidelines, all debts and taxes must be settled for the person who died. This includes water and electricity bills, credit card loans and personal taxes[241]. These are taken from the funds of the deceased and have priority over the distributions of monetary funds prior to the distribution of liquid monetary funds to the inheritors of the estate. Furthermore, mortgages and car loans along with other secured debts must also be paid. In the event that secured debts can't be paid, Section 32 of the Administration of Estates Act 1925 allows that both the real and personal estate of the deceased are assets for payment of such debts[242]. Only after the payment of debts from the estate, can the assets and funds be distributed to the heirs of the estate[243].

When a Japanese national has passed away in Japan, according to Article 882 of the Japanese Civil Code, the inheritance shall commence immediately upon the death of the decadent[244]. The Japanese system is rather unique in that the creditors do not take from the estate of the debtor

[241] https://www.gov.uk/probate-estate/settling-debts-and-taxes

[242] Administration of Estates Act 1925
https://www.legislation.gov.uk/ukpga/Geo5/15-16/23/section/32

[243] https://www.legalandgeneral.com/insurance/over-50-life-insurance/later-life-planning/what-happens-to-debt-when-you-die/

[244] Japanese Civil Code - Article 882

but instead, under Japanese law, heirs inherit the assets and the debts as well. However, there is a way which allows an inheritor of an estate to renounce an inheritance through the family court in the event that if the amount of the debts is greater than the amount of assets, an heir may make a statement to the family court that they renounce the inheritance. A renunciation of an inheritance must, however, be stated to the family court within three months from the time that the inheritor becomes aware of the death of the decedent and of the fact that they are an heir to the estate[245].

When comparing the two situations of Japan and the United Kingdom, there are some similarities. The key similarity is that the creditors will not be out of pocket as both countries have measures put in place to ensure that creditors will not cease to receive payments once the debtor has passed away. However, a key difference between the countries is how this is dealt with. In regards to the United Kingdom, the creditors are prioritised as getting immediate payment prior to the distribution of the estate. Creditors are entitled to receive the full amounts owed immediately from the funding of the debtor's estate. This is a vast contrast from the Japanese method of dealing with the deceased debts, which allows the inheritors of the estate to inherit the debt along with the assets. Despite this key difference, the overarching goal of ensuring that a fair and orderly first priority is conducted, remains as a key point held by both jurisdictions.

Priority Law (Inheritors)

After the first instance of priority law has been dealt with in the United Kingdom and all taxes and debts have been

---

[245] https://meguro-inter-lawfirm.com/qa/

paid, the estate is usually distributed according to a will that is left by the deceased[246]. However, in the event that a will does not exist, statutory procedure governs how a will should be distributed. In this case, the most common procedure occurs if an estate is valued below £322,000, wherein the entire estate goes to the spouse, regardless of whether children exist[247]. Anything above this threshold is split between children. If there is no spouse or children, there is a specific order that is governed by Section 46 of the Administrations of Estates Act 1925 as to who will inherit the estate[248]. The specifics of these rules attempt to find any close living relative to pass the estate onto. Furthermore, unlike Japan, the United Kingdom has an approach to inheritance that does not include certain practices that result from the cultural emphasis of the family. Instead, the United Kingdom approach focuses on the spouse and blood relatives.

In Japan, inheritance can be partly dictated by the deceased party leaving a Yuigonsho(遺言書), which is the Japanese equivalent to a will. This allows for beneficiaries of the estate to be designated[249]. However, Japan has the unique situation of the law dictating that even if a will has been put in place, certain relatives are entitled to a share of the estate. One such example is displayed in Article 890 of the Japanese Civil Code which dictates that a spouse shall always be considered as an heir to an estate[250]. If a will has

---

[246] https://www.gov.uk/probate-estate/distribute-the-estate

[247] https://www.gov.uk/inherits-someone-dies-without-will/y/england-and-wales/yes/after-jul-2023/yes

[248] https://www.legislation.gov.uk/ukpga/Geo5/15-16/23/section/46

[249] https://www.nic-nagoya.or.jp/en/living-in-nagoya/living-information/living_information/2019/11281300.html

[250] Japanese Civil Code - Article 890

not been left, then the Civil Code dictates the distribution of assets. Aside from the spouse, legislation gives the child or children of the deceased priority. If no living children exist, then priority goes to other lineal descendants such as grandchildren. However, in the event that no lineal descendants exist, priority is given to lineal ascendants such as parents or grandparents. Finally, if both lineal ascendants and descendants are non-existent, then priority is given to the siblings of the deceased[251].

When comparing both Japan and the United Kingdom's priority law, in regards to the inheritors of the estate, both countries have similarities and differences. Both Japan and the United Kingdom have legislation that is to be put into place if there is an absence of a will. However, a major difference is that the legislation in the United Kingdom has little to no effect on who the inheritors of an estate are if a will is present. This is a stark contrast to Japan, where the Civil Code can state that certain parties are automatically to be considered heirs of an estate. Both systems also prioritise the spouse of the deceased but differ in their level of prioritisation. The Japanese cultural emphasis on harmony and a private family life, often leads to private agreements regarding estate distributions. In contrast to this, the United Kingdom has highly structured intestacy rules to provide standardised and rigid distribution of an estate.

Scenarios Where No Valid Inheritor Exists

In Japan, if a will has not been left and it is not apparent whether or not an heir exists, the Japanese Civil Code dictates the procedure that should be followed. Firstly, in

---

[251]https://www.nic-nagoya.or.jp/en/living-in-nagoya/living-information/living_information/2019/11281300.html

the instance of uncertainty regarding the existence of an heir, an estate should be treated as a judicial person under Article 951 of the Civil Code[252]. If this scenario occurs, the Japanese family court appoints an administrator of inherited property upon application and then gives a public notice that this has occurred[253]. In the event that a sudden heir comes forward, the judicial person of Article 951 of the Civil Code shall be deemed to not have been created, so long as this does not prevent the effect of acts conducted by the administrator of inherited property within their authority[254]. The authority of the administrator of the inherited property extinguishes once the heir accepts the inheritance[255].

In the event that an heir has not been found within two months of giving public notice, the administrator of the inherited property must give public notice to any and all inheritance obligees and donees to explain that a claim for performance should be made within a given specified period[256]. If the specified period expires and no heir has come forward, then the family court shall, upon application by the administrator of the inherited property, give a public notice stating that if any heir is present, they must assert their right within a fixed given period of six months or more[257]. In the event that no person asserts their right as an heir within the given period, they forfeit the ability to exercise their right as an heir[258].

---

[252]Japanese Civil Code - Article 951

[253]Japanese Civil Code - Article 952

[254]Japanese Civil Code - Article 955

[255]Japanese Civil Code - Article 956

[256]Japanese Civil Code - Article 957

[257]Japanese Civil Code - Article 958

In the event that the six month period has gone by and any unknown heirs have now forfeited their right as heirs, applications may be made by 'a person who shared a livelihood with the deceased, a person who contributed to the medical treatment and nursing of the deceased or any other person with a special connection with the deceased' to the family court to grant the remaining amount of inherited property after liquidation in whole or part to them. However, the family court must find it reasonable and the application must be made within three months of the forfeiture of the rights of any unknown heirs[259]. Finally, any inherited property that has not been disposed of according to the rules set in the civil code, shall belong and become property of the National Treasury[260].

The Japanese system places a heavy emphasis on making sure that the rightful heirs are located and is very flexible with allowing heirs to come forward later on and petition for a claim to the state, which shows the emphasis within Japanese society on the lineage of the family.

In the United Kingdom, if a death occurs with no will or known heirs present, the case is dealt with by the Bona Vacantia team of the Government Legal Department[261]. However, they refuse to deal with insolvent estates and leave it for the creditors to sort out on their own[262]. In the event that a non-insolvent person dies and meets the

---

[258]Japanese Civil Code - Article 958-2

[259]Japanese Civil Code - Article 958-3

[260]Japanese Civil Code - Article 959

[261]https://www.gov.uk/government/organisations/bona-vacantia

[262]https://www.gov.uk/guidance/refer-a-deceased-persons-estate-to-the-treasury-solicitor

criteria to be dealt with by the Bona Vacantia team, members of the public may apply as an heir if they believe that they are a potential beneficiary to an estate. Usually, the potential beneficiaries are expected to support their own claim by production of evidentiary materials using a specialist genealogist[263].

There are set time limits when it comes to applying to the Bona Vacantia team. Claims will be accepted and paid with interest in the event that they are made within twelve years from the date upon which the estate administration was completed. After this time, claims will be accepted without interest being paid up until 30 years of the death of the deceased. However, after 30 years, no claims will be considered [264]. In the event that the time period elapses and no heir to the estate can be found, the estate becomes the property of the Crown[265].

The British system places a heavy emphasis on ensuring that ample time is given to make sure that any plausible heirs can come forward and try to make a claim. The hesitancy to return the land to the crown within a few years or as quickly as possible is a display of the importance of balancing the position of the crown and ensuring the use of land with respect for a private person's right to property.

When comparing the two nations, many similarities and differences come to light when dealing with situations where there is no apparent heir to an estate. One such similarity is that in both nations, they make an effort to attempt to find any possible heir before considering

---

[263]https://www.thegazette.co.uk/all-notices/content/103809

[264]https://www.thegazette.co.uk/all-notices/content/103809

[265]https://www.gov.uk/government/organisations/bona-vacantia

further options. However, the scope of this is different as it is much quicker for the chance to claim as an heir to expire in Japan than it is in England. Both countries also return the land to the state in the instance that an inheritor cannot be found, however, in the case of the United Kingdom it becomes property of the Crown. One key difference between the nations is how the governance of situations with estates where there are no apparent heirs is dealt with. In Japan, these situations are dictated almost wholly by the Japanese Civil Code, whereas in the United Kingdom, a much more flexible approach is in place where people are actively encouraged to consult with professional genealogists to find a connection with a long distance relative even though this is not written in statute.

Jus Accrescendi

Jus Accrescendi is a Latin term, meaning the right of survivorship. In regards to property law, this term refers to the events when land or a property is distributed as a usually equal stake amongst inheritors and in the unfortunate event that an inheritance dies, the stake is distributed amongst the remaining inheritors.

In the United Kingdom, Jus Accrescendi is put into place when a property is given in joint tenancy to multiple inheritants. This means that each owner is given an indivisible share in the property. When this happens and one of the inheritors passes away, the share that they owned is equally divided to the remaining co-owners of the property. This continues until there is only one owner of the property and upon the last persons death, it is classified as part of their own estate to be left to somebody in their will or the property can be sold by the last survivor[266].

---

[266]https://www.rochelegal.co.uk/news/owning-property-jointly-what-it-means/

It is also important to note that the right of survivorship cannot be altered by the rules of intestacy or by a will as the deceased inheritor would not have had a true identifiable share in the property. Therefore, upon an inheritor's death, the interest in the property cannot be transferred to another relative in a will as it will be overridden by the right of survivorship[267].

In contrast to this, Japan does not generally recognise the right of survivorship under Japanese law. This is as the rules of inheritance should be dictated by the civil code, which does not directly mention the right to survivorship as a concept. However, Japan does generally permit succession in co-ownership and allow that if an inheritor has no successors, then the other co-owners inherit the interest of the deceased[268]. In the event of a situation where the right of survivorship would apply in the United Kingdom, in Japan, the interest in the property would be subject to the same regulations as a normal death under the Civil Code.

The procedures in each opposing country are very different. The United Kingdom handles the situation in such a way, as to avoid future confusion and shares in a property being endlessly divided between the children of inheritors. In contrast to this, Japan has a system which holds the laws in the Civil Code as supreme and ensures an equal and fair distribution amongst relatives in the event of an inheritor's death. Both nations have disadvantages and advantages to the way they operate this. For example, the United Kingdom's implementation of Jus Accrescendi

---

[267]https://www.co-oplegalservices.co.uk/media-centre/articles-oct-dec-2019/right-of-survivorship-explained/

[268]https://nysba.org/NYSBA/Sections/International/Seasonal%20Meetings/Tokyo%202019/Coursebook/M%20Shikuma%20-%20Cross-Border%20Estate%20Planning%20in%20Japan.pdf

prevents heavy dilution of interests in a property and keeps things simple and easy for the law to understand in the events of disputes over inheritors deaths but it sacrifices a degree of empathy and fairness, whereas Japan ensures that families do not lose their entitled interest in a property in the event that the person holding an interest in the property dies but at the cost of judicial easiness and allowing many people to hold an interest in the property.

Conclusion

In conclusion, by taking a look into the situation that was discussed, it becomes obvious that not only the legal history but also cultural and societal values affect the outcome of how each nation deals with its respective cases. The inheritance laws of Japan are deeply rooted in equal distribution and a heavy respect for the lineage of a family, while at the same time, thinking about the benefits to the society which are possible while upholding the guidelines that are set in the Civil Code. On the other hand, the United Kingdom bases its inheritance laws on practical considerations and attempts to streamline procedures while also allowing the deceased party to have much more freedom regarding what they choose to do with their estate in their will which reflects the desire of the government not to impose too heavily on the personal affairs of a family.

www.ingramcontent.com/pod-product-compliance
Lightning Source LLC
Chambersburg PA
CBHW050319230526
45471CB00005B/2265